HOW TO STUDY SUCCESSFULLY

for better exam results

MICHELE BROWN read History at St Anne's College, Oxford. After teaching and working with an electronics company she spent some years as a reporter and script-writer for both television and radio.

She now concentrates on writing books. These include *How to Interview and be Interviewed* (Sheldon), biographies of Elizabeth II, Prince Charles and the Princess of Wales, and several anthologies of women's wit and humour.

Michèle Brown is married to Gyles Brandreth, and they have three children.

Overcoming Common Problems Series

Beating Job Burnout
DR DONALD SCOTT

Beating the Blues
SUSAN TANNER AND JILLIAN BALL

Being the Boss
STEPHEN FITZSIMON

Birth Over Thirty
SHEILA KITZINGER

Body Language
How to read others' thoughts by their gestures
ALLAN PEASE

Bodypower
DR VERNON COLEMAN

Bodysense
DR VERNON COLEMAN

Calm Down
How to cope with frustration and anger
DR PAUL HAUCK

Comfort for Depression
JANET HORWOOD

Common Childhood Illnesses
DR PATRICIA GILBERT

Complete Public Speaker
GYLES BRANDRETH

Coping Successfully with Your Child's Asthma
DR PAUL CARSON

Coping Successfully with Your Child's Skin Problems
DR PAUL CARSON

Coping Successfully with Your Hyperactive Child
DR PAUL CARSON

Coping Successfully with Your Irritable Bowel
ROSEMARY NICOL

Coping with Anxiety and Depression
SHIRLEY TRICKETT

Coping with Cot Death
SARAH MURPHY

Coping with Depression and Elation
DR PATRICK McKEON

Coping with Stress
DR GEORGIA WITKIN-LANOIL

Coping with Suicide
DR DONALD SCOTT

Coping with Thrush
CAROLINE CLAYTON

Curing Arthritis – The Drug-Free Way
MARGARET HILLS

Curing Arthritis Diet Book
MARGARET HILLS

Curing Coughs, Colds and Flu – The Drug-Free Way
MARGARET HILLS

Curing Illness – The Drug-Free Way
MARGARET HILLS

Depression
DR PAUL HAUCK

Divorce and Separation
ANGELA WILLANS

The Dr Moerman Cancer Diet
RUTH JOCHEMS

The Epilepsy Handbook
SHELAGH McGOVERN

Everything You Need to Know about Adoption
MAGGIE JONES

Everything You Need to Know about Contact Lenses
DR ROBERT YOUNGSON

Everything You Need to Know about Osteoporosis
ROSEMARY NICOL

Everything You Need to Know about Shingles
DR ROBERT YOUNGSON

Everything You Need to Know about Your Eyes
DR ROBERT YOUNGSON

Family First Aid and Emergency Handbook
DR ANDREW STANWAY

Overcoming Common Problems Series

Feverfew
A traditional herbal remedy for migraine
and arthritis
DR STEWART JOHNSON

Fight Your Phobia and Win
DAVID LEWIS

Getting Along with People
DIANNE DOUBTFIRE

Goodbye Backache
DR DAVID IMRIE WITH COLLEEN
DIMSON

Helping Children Cope with Divorce
ROSEMARY WELLS

Helping Children Cope with Grief
ROSEMARY WELLS

How to be a Successful Secretary
SUE DYSON AND STEPHEN HOARE

How to Be Your Own Best Friend
DR PAUL HAUCK

How to Control your Drinking
DRS W. MILLER AND R. MUNOZ

How to Cope with Stress
DR PETER TYRER

**How to Cope with Tinnitus and Hearing
Loss**
DR ROBERT YOUNGSON

How to Cope with Your Child's Allergies
DR PAUL CARSON

How to Cure Your Ulcer
ANNE CHARLISH AND DR BRIAN
GAZZARD

How to Do What You Want to Do
DR PAUL HAUCK

How to Enjoy Your Old Age
DR B. F. SKINNER AND M. E.
VAUGHAN

How to Get Things Done
ALISON HARDINGHAM

How to Improve Your Confidence
DR KENNETH HAMBLY

How to Interview and Be Interviewed
MICHELE BROWN AND GYLES
BRANDRETH

How to Love a Difficult Man
NANCY GOOD

How to Love and be Loved
DR PAUL HAUCK

How to Make Successful Decisions
ALISON HARDINGHAM

How to Move House Successfully
ANNE CHARLISH

How to Pass Your Driving Test
DONALD RIDLAND

How to Say No to Alcohol
KEITH McNEILL

How to Spot Your Child's Potential
CECILE DROUIN AND ALAIN DUBOS

How to Stand up for Yourself
DR PAUL HAUCK

**How to Start a Conversation and Make
Friends**
DON GABOR

How to Stop Feeling Guilty
DR VERNON COLEMAN

How to Stop Smoking
GEORGE TARGET

How to Stop Taking Tranquillisers
DR PETER TYRER

How to Stop Worrying
DR FRANK TALLIS

Hysterectomy
SUZIE HAYMAN

If Your Child is Diabetic
JOANNE ELLIOTT

Jealousy
DR PAUL HAUCK

Learning to Live with Multiple Sclerosis
DR ROBERT POVEY, ROBIN DOWIE
AND GILLIAN PRETT

Overcoming Common Problems Series

Living Alone – A Woman's Guide
LIZ McNEILL TAYLOR

Living Through Personal Crisis
ANN KAISER STEARNS

Living with Grief
DR TONY LAKE

Living with High Blood Pressure
DR TOM SMITH

Loneliness
DR TONY LAKE

Making Marriage Work
DR PAUL HAUCK

Making the Most of Loving
GILL COX AND SHEILA DAINOW

Making the Most of Yourself
GILL COX AND SHEILA DAINOW

Managing Two Careers
How to survive as a working mother
PATRICIA O'BRIEN

Meeting People is Fun
How to overcome shyness
DR PHYLLIS SHAW

Menopause
RAEWYN MACKENZIE

The Nervous Person's Companion
DR KENNETH HAMBLY

Overcoming Fears and Phobias
DR TONY WHITEHEAD

Overcoming Shyness
A woman's guide
DIANNE DOUBTFIRE

Overcoming Stress
DR VERNON COLEMAN

Overcoming Tension
DR KENNETH HAMBLY

Overcoming Your Nerves
DR TONY LAKE

The Parkinson's Disease Handbook
DR RICHARD GODWIN-AUSTEN

Say When!
Everything a woman needs to know about
alcohol and drinking problems
ROSEMARY KENT

Self-Help for your Arthritis
EDNA PEMBLE

Sleep Like a Dream – The Drug-Free Way
ROSEMARY NICOL

Solving your Personal Problems
PETER HONEY

Someone to Love
How to find romance in the personal columns
MARGARET NELSON

A Special Child in the Family
Living with your sick or disabled child
DIANA KIMPTON

Stress and your Stomach
DR VERNON COLEMAN

Think Your Way to Happiness
DR WINDY DRYDEN AND JACK GORD

Trying to Have a Baby?
Overcoming infertility and child loss
MAGGIE JONES

What Everyone Should Know about Drugs
KENNETH LEECH

Why Be Afraid?
How to overcome your fears
DR PAUL HAUCK

Women and Depression
A practical self-help guide
DEIDRE SANDERS

You and Your Varicose Veins
DR PATRICIA GILBERT

Your Arthritic Hip and You
GEORGE TARGET

Overcoming Common Problems

HOW TO STUDY
SUCCESSFULLY
for better exam results

Michèle Brown

SHELDON PRESS
LONDON

First published in Great Britain 1990
Sheldon Press, SPCK, Marylebone Road, London NW1 4DU

British Library Cataloguing in Publication Data
Brown, Michèle
    How to study successfully for better exam results. –
    (Overcoming common problems).
    1. Study techniques
    I. Title   II. Series
    371.30281

    ISBN 0–85969–615–4

Photoset by Deltatype Ltd, Ellesmere Port, Cheshire
Printed in Great Britain by Courier International Ltd, Tiptree, Essex

Contents

Introduction   1

1   Assessing Strengths and Weaknesses   5

2   Motivation   9

3   Choosing the Right Study Options   21

4   Working Conditions   23

5   Getting Organized   26

6   Concentration   31

7   Learning and Remembering   34

8   Effective Reading   39

9   Making Notes and Taking Notes   46

10   Essays and Written Work   52

11   Revision Techniques   70

12   Coping with Anxiety and Stress   74

13   Exam Techniques   82

14   After the Exams   88

15   How Parents Can Help   91

16   Useful Information   94

Introduction

What can one book teach which will assist all sorts of people with a wide range of age groups and abilities, studying a variety of different topics, for a number of different examination boards?

It certainly cannot teach you about all the individual quirks of every existing exam paper, still less what has to be learned for every subject. What it *can* do is teach you something so fundamental that it is relevant whatever your age group and whatever you are learning. It can teach you *HOW* to study.

Effective methods of study, good study habits and the right way to tackle examinations are mechanical skills which can be learned just as you can learn to swim or drive a car. They do not depend on intellectual brilliance but they can, on a similar principle to the story of the tortoise and the hare, help those who have learned them to succeed better than people who rely on natural ability alone.

The knowledge that you can maximize your potential by grasping a few simple basic techniques should begin to boost your confidence at once. This confidence, which will grow as you feel increasingly that you are working the right way, will be a major factor in getting the better exam results you are aiming for.

Perhaps you are reading this book because you are just starting on a course of study and you want to go about it in the most productive way possible. Maybe you have failed examinations or have achieved poor results and cannot understand why since you have been working hard. Perhaps you are being nagged by parents to do better than you think you can. Possibly you have great natural ability and do not think you are doing as well as you should. Whatever the reason there is no doubt that by learning to study in the correct way you can improve your results. The very fact that you have realized you *can* learn to study more effectively is a good indication that you are going to succeed.

The majority of students wanting a book on study techniques will be at school and studying for GCSE or A levels. But not all school students have teachers who make a specific attempt to teach students *how* to study (often because they have so much else to get through). This book is written so that students can use it by themselves, in addition to any guidance they get from school. It is presented in a straightforward way and can be used profitably by anyone working for exams at school.

It is also suitable for university and college students, and in particular for those who were not taught good study methods at school.

Teachers at universities and colleges frequently complain that the first thing they have to teach is nothing to do with the degree or diploma course. Instead they spend valuable time showing people how to work, get organized, concentrate and even how to write, construct grammatical sentences and spell! The methods advised in this book will help university and college students who, possibly for the first time, are organizing their own time and studies without the close supervision of the classroom.

Mature students and those studying for professional exams such as accountancy, law, local government or banking, also need to learn how to organize an efficient study programme.

If you did not develop good writing skills, learn how to organize yourself and your studies, and master exam and project techniques while you were still in full time education this book provides a simple and fundamental guide. It is not based on elaborate theories but offers down-to-earth, commonsense methods presented in a clear and uncomplicated way.

Many people believe they have worked very hard. They are hurt or mystified when it does not seem to pay off and they constantly fail or do badly. Usually this is because they put in the hours but do not know how to organize their time and work productively. Inability to concentrate during study time makes the number of hours irrelevant. Learn how to focus your attention on the task in hand and you will achieve more in less time. That is because your study time becomes, to use a piece of jargon, *quality time*.

With organization and concentration you will be able to achieve better results with less apparent work. However, if you

2

are going to do the job at all you may as well set out to do the best you can and that means getting actively involved in learning. It does not mean working long hours for the sake of it or sitting passively in front of notes without absorbing what they say. It means giving the task in hand – passing the exams or learning whatever would be useful to you – your best efforts and using energy to learn. Few people achieve good results without hard work, although many try to give that impression!

This book is about the three essentials that are relevant to all areas of study by all types of people – organization, concentration and hard work. It sounds daunting at first but once you have mastered the approach study will become simpler, less tiring and more satisfying.

Read the book through quickly to get an overall idea of its basic approach. Then go back and concentrate on the sections that are most appropriate to you. Follow the advice given as exactly as possible making necessary adjustments to fit your own particular circumstances and the subjects you are studying.

With just a little effort and careful planning you can certainly learn to study well enough to achieve your own personal goals. You will probably be pleasantly surprised to find you have more free time and less anxiety as well.

1

Assessing Strengths and Weaknesses

People's personalities and abilities differ. If you have a clear picture of what you are good at you can build on this knowledge and construct a choice of subjects and a scheme of study that benefit from your strengths.

If you know your areas of weakness you can work at improving them. You can also avoid choosing subjects that require precisely the skills in which you are weakest.

Surprisingly few people have a clear idea of what they are really like. A little honest research can throw up some interesting clues and save you and your teachers a lot of time in the future.

If you find it hard to start this exercise you will find school/study reports are a useful guideline. It is also helpful if someone whose opinion you value compiles a list of your strengths and weaknesses and you compare their lists with yours.

Using strengths and weaknesses

1. Be aware of weaknesses
Be aware of your weaknesses and devise ways to overcome them.

- Think through and list your *weaknesses*. Possible points might be: poor organization; laziness; easily distracted; avoiding getting to grips with problems; assessing lowest point of concentration in the day; no clear aims to work towards; lack of self-confidence; poor handwriting; weak grammar, etc.

    When you receive marked work back from lecturers/ teachers pay attention to any comments. Do not take them as personal criticism but as constructive advice from which you can learn where your weaknesses lie. If you want to discuss them or to ask for help do so while the work is still fresh in the teacher's mind.

Take a look at work that got better marks than yours, and try to understand why. You will then have a better idea of how your work looks in relation to the other work that the teacher is seeing and it will give you a better understanding of your faults and weaknesses.

- Overcoming weaknesses is not easy, and no-one can really do it for you.

  Do not try to do everything at once. Concentrate on one problem at a time, for example, a tendency to take on too much and inability to say no when asked to join in social events.

  Recognizing your weakness is a major step to overcoming it. The next step is to stay aware of it. Try to be totally honest with yourself. Keep asking yourself if you have genuinely made an effort to put things right.

  If you have a friend to trust ask her or him to pull you up when you do certain things. Do not give them the whole list of your misdemeanours – that might be too much to handle. Ask for help with something simple such as 'Stop me if you think I'm getting involved with too many things this term. I really need to spend a bit more time studying.'

- Now the good news. The more effort you make to overcome your weaknesses the more you will actually begin to get satisfaction, if not actual pleasure, out of your studies. As you begin to enjoy a few successes you will be encouraged to make more effort, particularly if teachers start to appreciate your extra efforts and take you and your work a little more seriously.

2. Recognize your strengths

Recognize your strengths and learn how to use them.

- Think through and list your *strengths*. Possible points might be: fast worker; not easily discouraged; good handwriting;

assessing most efficient time in the day; imaginative work; retentive memory, etc.

3. Use what you have learned to help your choice of subjects

Make use of what you have learned to help your choice of subjects.

- If one of your strengths is that you pick up vocabulary easily you should consider a language as one of your options.
- If you do not like things mathematical avoid the statistics option on a geography paper and choose an option with more human interest.
- If you know you want to work in the field of medicine you must take science options and make a positive effort to like them and work at them, even if there are aspects of them you find difficult.
- If you are not good with your hands do not choose a CDT option, even if you think it would be useful knowledge. Go for something less practical such as history of art.

4. Use what you have learned to plan study time

Make use of what you have learned about yourself to plan study time.

- If one of your weaknesses is that you cannot work without seven hours sleep a night you should be organizing your working week so that this is possible even if it means changing your social habits.
- If one of your weaknesses is you cannot help being distracted by others you should arrange to work somewhere away from your friends when you need to concentrate on homework or learning.
- If one of your strengths is that you are most alert at the beginning of the day you should be planning to do the most difficult work then.

After you have been following the advice in this book for at least half a term do this exercise again. If you have been following the advice seriously you should be able to consider adding *motivation*, *organization* and *concentration* to your list of strengths.

2

Motivation

Getting motivated

1. Think positive

To achieve success you have to decide to succeed.

You have probably seen top tennis players 'psyching themselves up' during important matches. They tell themselves to concentrate and put more effort into what they are doing. This is because their coaches have shown them that approaching a difficult challenge with a very positive attitude is as important to success as being technically good at what you do. As often as not, when they have given themselves a good talking to they go on to turn defeat into victory.

Take the same positive approach to your own difficulties. Don't look at problems as automatic causes of failure but as challenges to be overcome.

Don't see difficulties – see opportunities.

2. Look to the future and set long-term goals

To succeed you have to decide what you want.

This is the fundamental key to being successful. It can set an almost 'magical' chain of events in motion because subconsciously everything you do afterwards will be contributing to your overall aim.

So if you want to be successful in study and exams you have to have a clear picture of what you want. This means defining what your goals are, not just having a vague idea that you would like things to go a bit better.

Visualization

This is a really useful technique to help you define your goals and to keep them in sight all the time, even when you are not consciously thinking of them.

You may have heard of people using visualization techniques when they have an illness. They literally try to think themselves better and to picture the illness being destroyed. Visualization is a powerful weapon in making your own willpower and determination function as effectively as possible.

Make a mind-picture of what you want and where you want to be. Do you want to be a journalist? Picture yourself in a newspaper office, picture yourself behind the editor's desk (you must not be self-deprecating when using this technique!), picture yourself going out and checking on stories or speaking to the camera as a television news reporter.

Do you want a high-powered business career? Imagine yourself going to business school, maybe a business school in America. Picture yourself working successfully for a large, high-powered company. Picture yourself taking important decisions and making successful choices. Picture yourself running a business of your own and being your own boss.

Focus on what you *really* want from life. It may be the first time you have ever addressed this question properly and you may find your mind shying away from coming to some real decisions. Make yourself follow your thoughts through and try to create a picture of yourself having achieved your aims and ambitions. This is not just a technique for earth-shattering and worldly ambitions – you may aim for a life in the countryside or the opportunity to help others. What matters is that it gives you a genuine incentive to get through the hurdles along the way.

Keep working on this picture until it becomes a part of your life and you can refer to it at will.

You will find that eventually your subconscious mind will accept this long-term view. You will start to act and make decisions based on it without fully realizing how it is happening. Everything you do will be subtly geared towards the long-term achievement of the future you have 'visualized'.

Write down your long-term goals

These may include gaining a university place, making a career as an accountant, getting out of the rut of your present job. Writing things down helps you to define and confront your goals. Look at what you have written from time to time to keep yourself on target.

Over a period your long-term goals may alter. That does not matter. They will have got you going and made you realize that *getting what you want* is largely a question of *knowing what you want*.

3. Set your interim goals

These will probably be the exams you need to pass and the qualifications you need to go further. Write them down so that you can refer to them and remind yourself of why you are working.

4. Set short-term goals

This really means getting your daily timetable planned and making lists (see Chapter 5 on getting organized).

Try and decide at the beginning of each day what *you* hope to have achieved by the end of it. Don't just let things happen to you.

5. Don't underestimate yourself

Aim to stretch yourself to the best of your ability. If you know you are inclined to underestimate yourself (see Chapter 1 on assessing your strengths and weaknesses) monitor your goals frequently to ensure they are set high enough.

6. Rethink old attitudes

Have you allowed yourself to get into an attitude rut? Have you started letting things just happen to you, assuming you have no control over them? Perhaps you find yourself saying some of these things, without stopping to think what they really mean to you and the way you work:

- I'm no good at exams.
- Work is boring.
- People will think I'm boring if I work hard.

- Women are no good at maths and science.
- History is no use to anyone.
- Why bother to learn French, everyone speaks English these days.
- There's no point in trying, that teacher doesn't like me.
- This course lasts for years, I'll never stick it out.

Do you find you are talking like this to other people so that you encourage each other to think it is 'uncool' to be good at study or to make an effort? If so you will find that your attitude is seeping into the way you do things and preventing you from doing your best.

It is often said that 'you are what you eat'. It is even truer to say that '*you are what you think*'. If you think in terms of failure you can be quite sure that failure will come your way. Happily the reverse is true. If you can just pull yourself up short and reverse your attitude you can reverse your luck. If you think in terms of success, success will eventually be yours.

If you are reading this book because you genuinely want to get better at studying and passing exams you are already beginning to develop a new, positive attitude.

You can make your attitude to study even more positive once you accept that success depends on you and no-one else. If *you* have defined your own aims and planned how to achieve them then the impetus to do well will come from you and will not feel like something imposed on you.

Do not worry about whether you have enough 'brains'. Few exams are beyond the capacity of anyone with an average intelligence. Far more important factors in success are the right attitude, hard work and concentration. These are things you can develop for yourself.

Try and put some *energy* into what you do. Energy is not just something you have or do not have. Many performers who have great charisma in front of an audience warm themselves up in the wings, literally jumping up and down to work up a sense of energy and excitement before walking out to face the crowds. You can do this yourself, sometimes literally, but more often just by talking yourself into a positive frame of mind before you do something. Do not sit down and be listless and beaten before you start. Try saying to yourself 'I can and I will'. It is a cliché but you will be surprised how well it works.

With energy and the right attitude you can change the way you do things. You can even change the direction of your life! But for the moment just concentrate on the basics:

- Decide you like studying.
- Decide you like the subjects you are studying.
- Decide to be positive about your work.

7. Recreate your image

Sometimes teachers (or others who can influence your future) have negative ideas about you and what you can achieve. This may be because of your poor performance in the past or because you have been showing a negative attitude to study.

If people have a poor opinion of you they will begin to assume that you will always perform badly in your studies and exams. This becomes a vicious circle. When people expect poor results from you you may tend to fulfil their expectations.

Decide to break the circle and change your image. Once their initial surprise has worn off teachers will usually respond enthusiastically to a genuine attempt to improve attitude and performance. Their encouragement can be a vital part of maintaining a new, positive attitude to study.

8. Coping with loss of motivation

Everyone experiences times when it just seems easier to give up.

If this book assumed that once you started to follow the advice it gives all would be plain sailing, with no moments of tiredness or self-doubt, it would be unrealistic and you would have no confidence in it.

It is very important to be aware that everyone has periods of self-doubt and lethargy. Then, when they happen to you, you will recognize them for what they are – temporary bad times that will go away again.

This is particularly important if you are the sort of all-or-nothing person who thinks that one lapse means you have lost the entire battle. Do not assume it is the end of the world if you find you are not keeping to all your good intentions. Forget yesterday's failures. Decide to make a fresh start from where you are today.

You can lose the momentum for studying in several ways.

A sense of failure or futility

You wake up one morning and feel overwhelmed by everything that still has to be done. Perhaps you have allowed a backlog of work to build up which hangs over you like a depressing cloud. There seems to be so much to do you wonder whether it is worth even starting.

You may have a rather gloomy feeling, and literally experience a sense of being 'heavy hearted'. Life only seems possible if you keep your head under the pillow.

Do not despair. This happens to everyone, even the most successful, optimistic types. The basic remedy is to come out from under the pillow and decide to do something about it rather than give in to it. You will immediately start to feel better because you are getting back in control.

There are some useful pointers for getting back on the right track. Give yourself a little thinking time, preferably away from your normal working environment. Ask yourself a few basic questions.

(a) Is there a physical cause?

Check first of all that lack of motivation is not due to physical causes. Tiredness in particular can make you feel irritable and depressed.

- Are you getting enough sleep?
- Are you getting enough exercise and fresh air?
- Are you eating properly and not relying on sugary snacks?
- Are you enjoying enough relaxation from work?
- Is drinking too much coffee preventing you from sleeping properly?

14

(b) Are you oppressed by a particular problem?

Often the inability to work is linked to one outstanding and rather daunting task. Probably one you have been putting off until you no longer have enough time left to get it completed on time.

If you have a major deadline you know you cannot meet take your courage in both hands and *reschedule* it. You may feel awkward but you will feel even more awkward if you do not complete it on time without giving any explanation.

- It is usually better to be quite straightforward when speaking to teachers and tutors about rescheduling work.
- If you start giving phoney excuses such as being ill you can further complicate your life and that can be even more depressing.
- Make an appointment to see the teacher (it is better than a hurried conversation at the end of the lesson).
- Be honest; say you have been having difficulty keeping to your timetable and ask for extra time.
- If you have been experiencing difficulties with the work this is the opportunity to ask for a little extra help or guidance.
- Make sure that the rescheduled date really does give you enough time to finish or you will soon be in trouble again.

Often the relief of facing up to the problem and making enough time to work is enough to make you feel better immediately. Having earned your reprieve get on with the work immediately, before opting out becomes a habit.

(c) Do you feel you have lost the ability to study?

Sometimes you find you cannot bring yourself to face up to all the work which has to be done. Just the thought of it makes you feel oppressed. If you allow the feeling to persist you will eventually find yourself so far behind with your work that you have a genuine, major crisis on your hands. Every 24 hours that goes by without any achievement or progress will make you feel even less able to start again.

Luckily once you recognize the problem you can usually solve it by adopting a softly, softly approach. If you keep doing something, however small, you will find you have lost less time than you thought. Even more important, by refusing to be overwhelmed totally you will find that you feel better sooner.

Most important of all *do not give up*. You can be quite sure that the sense of pointlessness will definitely go away, often just as suddenly as it descends.

Try a different approach.

- Forget for a while about the major tasks and the sheer volume of work to be dealt with. You will only be further depressed at your inevitable failure.
- Deal with one day at a time.
- Set yourself one small task at a time, perhaps something you would normally feel should be dealt with outside basic working hours. Here are some suggestions. You will have other, similar tasks which you will feel pleased to have done when you get through the difficult time.

  (a) Reorganize files or notes.
  (b) Clean and tidy your work area.
  (c) Go to the library and see what books are available for a particular project.
  (d) Take overdue books back to the library.
  (e) Write off for some project information.
  (f) Paste illustrations into projects.
  (g) Get your diary up to date.
  (h) Tidy drawers and bookshelves.
  (i) Make any phone calls that you have been putting off.
  (j) Do any 'housekeeping' tasks (shopping, meals for the freezer, ironing etc.) so that you have clear time when you get back to your timetable.

- Whatever happens try and achieve *something* so that the day does not feel wasted. A wasted day is very depressing when you are working towards a set goal.

- If you keep going on these minor tasks that do not require a high level of energy and enthusiasm, you will begin to feel much better. Before too long, maybe just a couple of days, you will be able to plan for more than a day at a time and will go back to being yourself.

A sudden sense of panic and inability to concentrate

This particular type of difficulty usually occurs when major deadlines or exams loom up (see Chapter 12 on coping with anxiety and stress).

As a general rule panic usually subsides once you actually sit down and start doing something. Start gently with something fairly mechanical which does not require real mental effort.

Creeping inertia and backsliding

Negative feelings about work are not always accompanied by depression or panic. Your good intentions can be eroded away slowly by carelessness and laziness, and a lot of effort is required to get back on the right path.

Perhaps you started to ignore your timetable or asked to copy someone else's notes because you could not be bothered to make your own, or you did not complete a particular essay on time. You and a friend agreed to revise and test each other but you did not bother because you do not have to answer to a friend in the same way as a teacher. Maybe you started to skip a class or two.

How can you cope with creeping failure to keep to your set tasks and goals before it ruins all your plans and leaves you thinking that you cannot manage? First, recognize you have a problem. Second, make a positive decision to deal with it. This can be hard, especially when you only have yourself to answer to. A study partnership with another student or group of students is a help if you are easily tempted into backsliding, because you will have to explain yourself to others.

Here are two questions to ask yourself.

- Are you getting towards the end of a long period of study? If so you are probably feeling stale. You simply have to recognize the fact that you may have periods of boredom and frustration, and decide not to give in especially if the end is in sight.

- Are you suffering from an overall lack of enthusiasm or are one or two specific subjects creating a problem which is having a bad effect on your whole work programme?

If you can pinpoint one or two areas where you are having fundamental problems then you can isolate them and deal with them. Once the trigger problems are sorted out you will probably find the rest falls into place.

Ask yourself why the problems have arisen.

Are you unhappy about the choice of subject? Do you feel you are putting in effort where it is being wasted? If so you must make a realistic assessment of whether or not it is possible, or even wise, to change subjects at this stage. To do your best work you must be convinced that you are doing the right thing or the incentive will not be there. Look again at Chapters 2 and 3 on motivation and choosing the right subjects.

Do you have a personality clash with the teacher concerned which is making you unwilling to work? If so is it possible to change groups? Alternatively you should try and take an objective look at your own attitude and see if by being more positive you could change the teacher's attitude to you.

Are you feeling resentful of the amount of time spent studying? Look at your timetable. Did you set yourself an impossibly demanding work schedule so that inevitably you were bound to be overwhelmed?

See if you can rework your timetable, make it more realistic so that you have time to relax. If your work schedule is still too heavy then consider dropping or postponing one of the subjects. This should be a last resort but it is preferable to putting your entire study plan at risk.

Do you feel there is no point to what you are doing? Do you feel resentful of the time you are studying and desperate to cut corners?

Look again at your overall goals. Go back to square one and

look at *why* you are working, what you hope to achieve in the long run. Try to keep this broad aim in view and not lose sight of it by getting bogged down in day-to-day detail and worry. Look to the future, when you have got through this difficult phase and you have achieved what you wanted. Reaffirm what you want and then make a deliberate effort to get back to working properly so that you can achieve it.

The following are some useful ideas to think over.

I can and I will. In other words 'think positive'. When you find the old negative thoughts creeping in make a conscious effort to recognize them and reject them. It really is up to you.

This is a surprisingly effective sentence to say to yourself when things seem too difficult to cope with.

If a job's worth doing it's worth doing badly. This is another useful phrase to keep in your mind when things start to overwhelm you. It does not mean that you can now go away and do everything as badly as you like. But when you begin to feel overwhelmed by everything you have to do (and this usually happens to people with very high personal standards, who perhaps take everything a little too seriously) then it is better to lower your standards a little and just get the job done. After all it is better to have something to show at the end of the day rather than nothing at all.

You will probably find that if setting your standards too high is preventing you from achieving then just breaking through and starting to work, even if you are not totally satisfied with the results, is the start of curing the problem.

Thinking time

There is just a chance that you are getting unnecessarily anxious about your work rate because you feel you should always be *doing* something.

Although you should have a full timetable and stick to it remember that there is a value to thinking. If you are taking time to mull things over or let thoughts settle in your head before writing an essay that does not mean you are not working properly.

When people joke about having their best ideas while soaking in the bath there is a lot of truth in what they say. It is often a good idea to do the preliminary work on a project, essay or set of notes and then take some thinking time before putting pen to paper. Your brain will then continue a subconscious process of sorting and sifting while you get on with doing something quite different.

Another worthwhile approach is to take a question or proposition and give yourself a set space of time in which to sit and simply think it through from every possible angle. This will prevent you from always writing the first thing that comes into your head and will help you to develop a logical way of thinking problems through.

So just because you are not spending every moment with a pen in your hand do not assume that you have lost the ability to work. Thinking things over is a *most important* part of your work. (But don't make 'thinking' an excuse for simply staring into space and avoiding work!)

9. Reward yourself

Making yourself miserable is not the key to successful study. It is important to keep yourself happy. As well as defining your goals give yourself minor incentives of rewards and treats (an evening out with friends, time to relax with a book or the television) when you have been working hard or when you complete a stretch of work.

Be kind to yourself without feeling guilty. Simple day-to-day incentives will stop you feeling stale and resentful of time spent studying. Leisure time and interests should be a part of all your planning.

3

Choosing the Right Study Options

Choosing the subjects most suited to your abilities, and the subjects that will help you with your plans for the future, is a very important factor in providing the motivation you need to study effectively.

- If you are taking GCSE you will know that English and maths are essential for almost any future study or employment. Also advisable are a foreign language and a science.
- If you are going on to do A levels or any type of further or higher education then you should discuss the choice of additional GCSE subjects with a teacher or tutor, so that you choose the correct combination.
- When choosing A levels you should discuss with a teacher or tutor whether the choice will qualify you for the higher/further education, professional qualification or job you plan to go on to.
- If you are studying on your own without professional help then be sure to check that you are studying the right subjects for the career or further education you are aiming for.

  (a) Send off for the prospectus of the college you are hoping to apply for and make a thorough check of the entry qualifications.
  (b) Get the regulations of the professional body you wish to join and check that you are following the right course.
  (c) Write to the personnel department of the company you wish to join and ask about educational requirements.

- Where a choice of subjects is available then choose the subject you like best; this will immediately increase your chances of success.

- Where you have to do a subject in which you are weak remember that a new, confident approach will increase your chances of success. Don't get off to a bad start by talking yourself into failure. Stop immediately if you hear yourself saying things like 'I'm hopeless at maths', or 'I'll never be able to do French'.

Just as you can talk yourself into failure you can talk yourself into success. Keep telling yourself you *can* do it, you *will* succeed, nothing is too difficult.

4

Working Conditions

Your ability to work effectively will be much greater if you organize the best working conditions you can. You do not need a luxurious office in order to work effectively. However, if you get a few basic essentials right you will achieve better results from the time you put into your study.

Basic essentials

1. A working area without distractions

Although some people claim they work better with background music it is generally accepted that people concentrate best in an environment where there are no other people talking, no radio or television and no interruptions.

If your entire home is a distraction (this will particularly apply to mature students with domestic responsibilities) try to spend some study time in a library or in someone else's house where you have no responsibilities.

2. Furniture

Get a desk

This need not be expensive. You can make a simple trestle table relatively cheaply, or buy an old kitchen table at a house sale. But make sure (a) that it is big enough to spread out your papers; and (b) that it is just for you, so you can leave projects and books on it, undisturbed, between study sessions.

Get a chair

The chair should be comfortable and supportive and suit the height of the desk. Do not use a chair that leaves you slumped over your work. Poor posture at the desk will prevent your lungs from working efficiently and will put a strain on your back.

3. Good lighting

A good quality desk light is an invaluable aid. Buy the best you can afford. An adjustable one is best; it may be expensive but it will last for years. Regard it as an investment in your future because it will make studying less tiring and will make you work more efficiently.

Use some general room lighting as well as the desk light. This will be more comfortable for your eyes.

4. Storage space

The basics are:

- book shelves (planks on bricks if necessary)
- drawers or boxes for keeping paper and clutter
- a good-sized wastepaper basket – a large cardboard box will do very well.

Adequate storage space will help you get into a routine of being tidy. Being tidy will make study infinitely easier, quicker and more productive than studying surrounded by chaos.

At the end of a study session do not go away leaving everything just as it is. Tidy up: throw away waste paper; put things into your bag ready for the next day; put books away tidily on shelves; put pens and pencils in a jar; tick off what you have done from your list; leave everything ready for a fresh start.

Do all this at the end of a study session rather than wasting valuable time tidying up at the beginning when you are freshest and best able to study.

5. The right equipment

What do you need? Books, paper, pens, dictionary, calculator, atlas? Whatever you need on a day-to-day basis should be ready to hand. Why waste time looking for things when you can have everything ready and waiting? Wouldn't you rather spend the time watching your favourite TV programme or seeing friends than searching for missing notes, books, pen refills or scissors?

6. The right physical conditions

You will need enough warmth to be comfortable. Too much heat will make you sluggish and drowsy.

You will need adequate fresh air as your brain functions better with a good supply of oxygen, so try to have a window open.

Even in cold weather let fresh air into the room from time to time.

5

Getting Organized

Organizing your study habits will lead to immediate improvement. How much time and effort do you waste at the moment by forgetting the things you need for a particular lesson, forgetting when the homework should be finished, losing notes, etc.?

If you are disorganized in every job you do, even something done on a regular basis has to be started from scratch. That means a lot of unnecessary, repetitive hard work and a greater possibility of failure if you become discouraged.

Get organized; your standard of work will go up and you will find you have time to spare instead of always being in a state of panic.

The basics of organization

1. Make lists

This is probably the most valuable new habit you can learn.

- List everything you have to do; a shorthand notebook is the ideal place to keep lists.
- Keep separate lists for things you have to do that are not study-related. This will help you with general organization. Put time aside to deal with things on the general list rather than constantly getting distracted when you should be studying.
- Cross things off your list when you have done them. This gives a motivation in itself; you will find that crossing completed tasks off the list is very satisfying!

2. Use a diary

A diary is an invaluable tool to help you organize your time productively. When your diary is well organized you will not waste time forgetting things or worrying about forgetting things.

- Keep only one diary; that way you can relax knowing it has everything in it.
- Use a diary which is not too large, so that you can take it with you everywhere you go.
- A diary where you can see the week at a glance, on a double-page spread, is probably the most useful.
- A more useful diary is one that runs from the start of the academic year rather than the calendar year (these are available).
- Fill in all long-term information (exam dates, holiday dates, etc.) as soon as you get the diary.
- Fill in information you may need while you are away from home (telephone numbers, addresses, etc.).
- Fill in new arrangements (appointments, meetings, dates when library books should be returned, etc.) as soon as you make them.
- Make a note of deadlines in the diary. If you always leave things to the last moment cheat on yourself by bringing deadlines forward and writing in warnings of approaching deadlines a few days ahead.
- Keep your diary neat and up to date; use correcting fluid to blank out anything that needs to be changed.
- Use an elastic band round the front cover and used pages, so that the diary opens at the current week.
- Stick an envelope inside the back cover so that you can keep things like tickets and appointment cards in it.
- Personal planners (filofaxes) which have room for notes, addresses etc. are also available. Obviously they are smarter than a diary with an envelope in the back and this may encourage you to be better organized. However they are more expensive, and it is quite possible to be well organized without one.
- Look at your diary at the end of every day. Make sure you know what is happening the next day. Is everything ready? Have you done any necessary preparation? Do you have everything you are going to need?

3. Use card index files

Card indexes are the small boxes that take record cards, and that can be divided up, usually alphabetically. There are two standard sizes; the larger size, which takes 152×102 mm ($6'' \times 4''$) record cards is most useful.

If you want to divide the sections into your own categories you can simply put sticky labels over a set of alphabetical dividers and write your own headings.

Card indexes are a wonderfully flexible way of adding to information as you go along. Use them:

- for keeping your own personal list of useful names, and sources of information
- to build up your own 'indexes' of information, such as book lists
- to keep information for projects and extended course work well organized.

For example, if you are doing a project on a topic such as *inner cities* you can build up the information as your research progresses, making notes on sources of information or noting down individual useful facts under headings such as housing, transport, local government, crime, employment, cities in the United States, etc.

Card indexes not only help you keep all your information safely and give you a safe place for keeping isolated snippets of information. As you keep returning to the index to add extra information you will also get a clearer picture of how the information could be organized when you finally come to write up the project in full.

4. Make timetables

Timetables will help you get the most out of the time available. They bring a purposeful structure to your day. When you make them take into account that you can work better at certain times in the day.

Planning a timetable

- Your timetable will depend entirely on your individual schedule. The whole point of making a timetable is to organize your own time to accommodate your own particular requirements, circumstances and methods of working.

- Work out how much time you need to study by yourself in addition to lesson time. Your teachers will probably help, either by giving you a homework schedule or by indicating how much time you should be spending on each subject per week.

- Timetables should include time not only for writing essays, making notes, projects etc. but also *for learning new work*. This may not be included by teachers in homework timetables, but it is essential if you are to learn new facts as efficiently as possible (see p. 38, 6 Steps to Thorough Learning).

- If you are studying alone, or by correspondence course, follow the guidelines given by tutors. List the amount of work you are required to produce at the end of a week. Calculate how long it will take to do. This plus learning time is the amount of time that should be covered by your study timetable.

- Divide the time available into working sessions of 30–45 minutes, depending on your own concentration span (the older the student the longer the concentration span).

- Allocate working sessions for each subject and for learning time. Try and keep to a regular timetable without making changes, as a familiar routine makes working easier.

- Include time for meals.

- Include times for exercise/fresh air at regular intervals.

- Organize key work for times when you are at peak efficiency.

- Keep background work and relaxation for times when your concentration is at a lower ebb. (You should already be clear when you work best after doing the exercise of listing your strengths and weaknesses.)

- If you have other responsibilities and calls on your time either:

  (a) block off study time and plan a separate timetable for other tasks; *or* (b) do a full timetable to include time for these other commitments.

- Pin your timetable where you can see it easily.
- Use the timetable together with a list of tasks to be completed each day. As you finish each block of study tick it off the list and give yourself the satisfaction of knowing you are a little further towards achieving your ultimate goal.
- Do not cheat on your timetable. When you reach the end of time allocated to one task move on; come back to unfinished work later.
- Let your friends and family know when you have planned to study so they do not interrupt. You should also let them know when you are free or they might assume you are studying all the time and you would have no social life at all!

If you keep running out of time then your timetable needs reorganizing. Either you have not allocated enough time to each subject or you have become bogged down in timewasting study habits – see Chapter 6 on concentration, Chapter 8 on effective reading, and Chapter 9 on making and taking notes.

6
Concentration

Concentration is really a matter of getting your *mind* organized. Plan the work which needs to be done, allocate an adequate amount of time to complete it and then apply yourself to it *without allowing other things to distract you.*

If concentration is your major problem you will find that once you have sorted out your motivation and got yourself basically organized concentration should become noticeably less difficult.

However, you have to face the fact that concentration will not come automatically. It always takes a certain effort of will to apply your mind carefully to one particular task.

Steps towards concentration

1. Anxiety and stress
If you find that you have become so anxious about study that it is interfering with the very concentration you need to put things right, look at Chapter 12 on coping with anxiety and stress.

2. Remove distractions
- Deal with one subject at a time.
- Remove everything from the work area except what you are working on at the time. Remove other things from your desk and eyeline.
- Turn off the telephone or work where you cannot hear it.
- If you have something *really important* to do which is *really* nagging at you do it before you begin to study. But do not use trivial tasks as excuses for putting off getting on with the work.

If something important comes into your mind as you study write it down quickly on your list of things to do; this way you know you will remember to deal with it later. Meanwhile you can put it out of your mind until the study period is over.

If being away from your own home makes it easier to avoid distractions work in a library or in the home of an understanding friend.

3. Work in set timespans

- Try to concentrate closely for about 40 minutes at a time (or whatever you have decided is your ideal concentration span).
- If 40 minutes is too long to concentrate begin with 10 minute sessions and gradually lengthen the amount of time you can concentrate without allowing other thoughts to creep in. Aim for a minimum of 30 minutes as this will be better preparation for the extended concentration period of an exam question.
- After every session take a mini-break for a drink or short walk around.
- Every two sessions take a longer break to clear your mind. Use this time to do small tasks on your daily list such as making telephone calls, or go for a short walk and get some reviving fresh air.

4. Plan your work

- Work to a timetable based around your 30–40 minute attention spans.
- Make yourself a mini-timetable for one day, or one particular study session if necessary.
- Schedule your best subject first to ease yourself in.
- Schedule your worst subject second, before you get tired.
- Keep to your timetable.

5. Keep checking on yourself

Are you allowing your mind to wander? Is your brain skimming the surface of what you are reading rather than really committing it to memory? If so you are not gaining a great deal from what you are doing.

- Take a break, get some fresh air then start afresh and try and involve yourself in what you are doing.
- Keep asking yourself if you are *really* concentrating and whether you have gone on beyond the time when you can usefully work.

6. Express yourself clearly

Part of concentration is deciding not to be slapdash about presentation. If you aim for good presentation in your own notes as well as in work done for assessment it will help make study and concentration easier.

- If you have problems with spelling decide to put things right. Get a dictionary and use it.
- When you concentrate seriously on your work you will not be happy about sloppy grammar. Go to the library and find a book such as *How to Succeed in Written Work and Study* by Ellis and Hopkins. Look at the section that lists elementary mistakes and shows what is correct. Make sure you understand why you are getting things wrong and how you can put them right.

7. It gets better

- Concentration is a good habit that you can acquire with practice. The more you work at it the better it gets.
- If you are having trouble applying yourself to a particular topic remind yourself that the more you know about a subject the more interesting it becomes and the easier it is to concentrate.
- If you still cannot summon up enthusiasm take a look at your list of long-term goals. Remind yourself why you are doing this, quite apart from the intrinsic interest of the subject itself!

7

Learning and Remembering

Learning and remembering are skills you can teach yourself. Try and get into the habit of using facts and concepts like building bricks. Be patient. When one layer has been thoroughly established add another layer. Trying to do too much at once is counterproductive.

If you believe you have a block about learning certain subjects you will be pleasantly surprised to discover that simply deciding on a more positive attitude to learning is a major step to making remembering easier.

Learning methods

1. Learn by heart

This picturesque phrase means learning something so thoroughly it literally seems to become a part of you.

Learning by heart usually involves learning by repetition or reciting, without thinking too much about the meaning. It is the ideal method for basic facts that are the 'building bricks' of different subjects – formulae, grammar, vocabulary, dates, theorems.

There is nothing childish about learning things by rote and off by heart. Repetition is the surest way to achieve the 'overlearning' that ensures facts stick in your memory for a long time.

2. Understanding is the key to remembering

To learn something and be confident you can use it you must first have understood it properly. Always make sure you quite understand what you are trying to commit to memory. If you are not sure *ask* someone.

Never pretend you have understood when you have not, otherwise the next stage, which will build on what you are supposed to know and understand already, will be even harder and eventually you will not be able to make any progress.

3. Look for patterns

Seeing logical patterns in facts makes them much easier to understand and learn.

- Look for patterns or rhythms in verbs, lists and formulae; it makes it easier to learn these basic building bricks of information by heart.
- When authors write textbooks (or any other sort of book for that matter), they work to a logical plan. Additional information is added to a basic framework.
- Get into the habit of looking for this fundamental framework in information so that you do not see it as one indigestible mass (see also Chapter 9 on making and taking notes). You will find plenty of clues, and the more you get used to looking for them the easier it will become. Look first at chapter headings and subheadings to see where the writer is leading you. In very straightforward textbooks there may also be notes in the margins to draw your attention to the most important facts.
- If you are not working directly from a book you must put your own logical pattern into the information you are given. In lessons or lectures the person teaching you will have done this anyway, so again it is a question of looking out for something that already exists.
- Once you have the pattern of any sequence of facts or ideas clear in your mind you can then add extra information to it – like putting extra clothes into a well-organized storage cupboard.
- When you come to learn and revise your priority will be to grasp the basic patterns, plus whatever facts you need to back them up. After that it becomes a matter of how much more you think you want to add, or feel you can add, without losing your grasp of the logical pattern.

4. Active learning

Don't just read what you have to learn – that is too passive. Get *involved* in what you are learning.

- Say what you learn out loud, it helps you understand and remember.
- Explain what you have learned to someone else; you will soon find out if you have understood it clearly.
- Write summaries of topics when you think you have learned them.
- Make diagrams of what you have learned to show a logical sequence.
- Use a tape recorder to listen to yourself. Record your explanation of what you have learned and then play it back: does it make sense?
- Use a tape recorder to test yourself by, for example, recording foreign vocabulary while you are learning it. Leave gaps for the translation, and test yourself a few days later.
- Use a tape recorder to record quotations, formulae, legal definitions, dates etc. that need to be learned by heart. Play them to yourself when you are doing other things. You can use a Walkman personal hi-fi to do this on journeys and use the time usefully.
- Ask people to test you on what you have learned. It will also help you to learn if you test them.

5. Cultivate a 'photographic memory'

This method may not suit everyone but it is worth making some effort to master it. You may even find that you can memorize pages or even entire chapters in complete detail.

- Learn to look at a page and memorize it as one item; then try to recall the whole page at will and 'read' it.
- Naturally it takes practice to become good at this. Try recalling your own notes, which should be written in a way that you find particularly easy to memorize. Remember when

you are writing up notes that information presented interestingly is easier to recall.

6. Turn facts into pictures

Often it is easier to remember pictures rather than words.

- If you have to memorize any facts that lend themselves to being turned into diagrams or illustrations then use that method.
- Statistics and geographical information are obvious examples of facts that lend themselves to visual representation. Much scientific information is best presented and remembered as diagrams.
- Use illustration imaginatively as a learning tool. For example, memorize the events leading up to the Second World War by drawing a map of Europe and numbering in the right order the countries that Hitler invaded. When you need to remember it picture the map rather than trying to remember a list of names.

7. Use 'memory-joggers'

Write things to be learned by heart on cards, for instance quotations, scientific formulae, history dates, different tenses of verbs in foreign languages.

- Pin cards where you will constantly see them, such as on the bathroom mirror, on the notice board above your desk, by the kettle.
- Use cards in rotation so that they do not become 'stale'. Test yourself on the information when the cards are changed over.
- Keep cards in handbag, satchel or pocket. Look at them in your 'spare' time, such as when sitting on a bus.

8. Use memory aids (mnemonics)

Mnemonics are little tricks you play to help your memory. They might be easily remembered sentences where the first letter of each word is the first letter of a list. For example, *Richard Of*

York Gave Battle In Vain is a way of remembering that the colours of the spectrum are Red, Orange, Yellow, Green, Blue, Indigo and Violet; or short rhymes, for example:

> Professor Jones has gone below,
> We shall not see him more.
> For what he thought was H_2O
> Was H_2SO_4!

– a reminder of the difference between water and sulphuric acid!
– or familiar numbers, such as remembering the code for your padlock is the same as the date, month and year of your birth.

You can make up your own mnemonics. Use words where the letters are from the first words of lists you have to remember. Use names, birth dates etc. that have special meaning for you and are easy to remember.

9. Six steps to thorough learning

Whichever method you find most useful the following timetable for committing new information to memory definitely gets results.

(a) Learn new work using an appropriate method.
(b) Revise it again briefly the following day.
(c) Revise again about five days later.
(d) Revise again after a further five days.
(e) Test your knowledge (verbally or by writing it down).
(f) Revise again in the run-up to the exam.

8

Effective Reading

Do you find it takes you a long time to read books or notes that other people seem to skim through? Or that you can spend a long time reading a book and at the end of that time you remember almost nothing that was in it? Or that it is hard to work out whether a book will be useful to you without first reading the whole of it?

If the answer to any of these questions is 'yes' then you can definitely make your studying more effective by learning to read more efficiently.

You may think that reading is a straightforward skill you learned as a child. Either you can read or you cannot read. However reading abilities differ like everything else. Some people can read quickly automatically pitching the level of concentration at the level required by the particular book they are reading. Others waste hours plodding slowly, word by word through every book, whether it is a major textbook or a Barbara Cartland novel.

Not surprisingly, students who are slow readers panic about keeping up with the volume of work required. Yet recognizing the need to learn to read more quickly will lead to a rapid improvement both in reading speed and the ability to absorb relevant information.

Whole books have been written on the subject of rapid reading. You may like to borrow one from the library and go into the subject in detail but it probably is not necessary. The two most important facts to realize are:

- Reading faster is a matter of habit.
- Reading each individual word is not good work but a waste of time.

Bearing these two simple thoughts in mind, slow readers can improve in a matter of days with a little determined practice.

Pointers to better reading

1. Decide to read faster

First, and most important, begin to try to read faster, without even thinking about the method of achieving it.

2. Read for the overall sense

If you are still reading one word at a time you will see a sentence divided like this:

> As/the/second/course/was/brought/in/the/King's/Champion/
> Sir/Robert/Dymock/rode/into/the/hall/on/a/charger/and/
> offered/to/do/battle/on/the/King's/behalf.

Having read each word as a separate entity you then have to put them together again to make some sense of them. But people who read rapidly, read and make sense of the pattern of the words at the same time. They are more likely to see the same sentence in sections like this:

> As the second course was brought in/the King's Champion/Sir
> Robert Dymock/rode into the hall on a charger/and offered to
> do battle/on the King's behalf.

If a break in the sense comes after the beginning of a line the eye goes straight to that and does not bother to start at the beginning of the line each time. Really fast readers, reading on a topic with which they are very familiar, can read a book almost by looking down the middle of each page.

- Read not in single words but in groups of words, in phrases or even whole lines at a time.
- Read for the overall sense of what is being said.

- Aim to read fast and accurately.

3. Look for clues

Try to recognize the underlying framework of what you are reading and to identify the main points being made. It is particularly important to be able to do this without reading the whole book as often you will simply be assessing a book to see if it *might* be useful!

- Look first at the chapter headings of the book; this will give you an indication of the main areas covered.
- Look at the index to see what topics are covered in detail.
- Skim through each chapter or major section first, before you read it properly. This will give you an overall view of what it is all about. Do not attempt to make notes at this stage.
- Make use of 'clues' in the form of subheadings or short summaries in the margin.
- Begin reading once you have established a clear idea of the point of the book. You will find it infinitely easier to read a book quickly and understand it if you have already established some sense of what it is about. This is the point at which you should start to make notes if necessary.

4. Stop childish reading habits

Stop doing the things you did when you started to learn to read.

- Don't use your finger to point along the lines.
- Don't mouth the words.
- Don't read aloud.
- Don't keep looking back at words you have just read, keep looking at the words ahead.

All these habits slow you down by making you read one word at a time.

5. Read actively

Speed is not enough in itself; you must also understand what you read. Keep questioning all the time you are reading. This will keep your brain alert as you read. If you are taking notes it will help you formulate them properly.

- What is the author trying to say?
- Do you understand it well enough to explain to someone else?
- Can you spot any mistakes?
- Is there anything with which you disagree?

6. Improve your vocabulary

You may be a slow reader because you are unsure of the meanings of many of the words you come across. Improving your vocabulary takes work but your reading will become faster and more informative.

- Get a dictionary and use it to look up any word you do not know or are unsure of.
- Start a vocabulary book for all your new words. Keep a small notebook on you to learn words in spare moments.
- Keep a list of words that keep cropping up in a particular subject. Look them up or ask your teacher/tutor about their meaning.
- Allocate time each week in your timetable for learning new vocabulary.
- Get someone to test you.
- Use new words yourself. It has been shown that successful people have demonstrably larger vocabularies than others. Why not put yourself in the running for success by enlarging your own vocabulary?

7. Start a reading habit

- Read as much as possible. The more you read, whatever the subject, the more proficient and faster you will become.
- Read good writers. You will gain the extra benefit of absorbing some of their skills and good writing practices that may reflect in your own writing.
- Read for pleasure. When you are not studying you can relax

and be less intense about reading quickly and with concentration. However, do not lapse into reading word by word or even reading for relaxation will become hard work again.

8. Use the libraries

Libraries can be a great source of help and information. They can also be good places to escape to when you want peace and quiet or a change of environment.

- Make a conscious effort to use your school/college or local library. Your aim should be to feel totally at home in a library and using the information retrieval systems you find there.
- Walk around and locate the catalogues, the microfiche or microfilm machine, the shelves where the books about your particular subjects are stored, where the standard reference books such as dictionaries, *Who's Who*, *Whitaker's Almanack*, town directories, etc. are kept.
- Ask the librarian how to use the catalogue in order to locate particular books or areas of reference. Recently nearly all catalogues have gone over to microfiche and microfilm systems. Lists of books held by a particular institution or local authority will also be on a computer database, which may or may not be available to the general public. A few places still have the old card-index files.

  If you feel too shy/embarrassed to ask for a lesson in using the catalogue select one or two books you wish to locate and ask the librarian to help you find them. Use the opportunity to learn by observation and asking questions.
- To find books using the catalogue you need either author or title or subject matter. There are indexes of books under all three headings. For instance to find the book *Bluff Your Way in Ballet* by Craig Dodd you could do one of the following:

  (a) look up Dodd C. in the author index;
  (b) look up *Bluff Your Way in Ballet*, in the title index;
  (c) look up *Ballet* in the subject index; look at all the titles

listed until you find the title dealing with exactly the aspect of the subject you are interested in.

(Even when you know the title and author of a book it is useful to look in the subject index to see what other books there are on the same subject.)

Computer systems are becoming more sophisticated all the time. Learn to use them and they can save you hours of effort and improve the quality of your work by helping you to locate all the sources of information you need.

- Understand the classification system. The most common library classification system is the Dewey decimal system which is based on numbers. Basic subject numbers are to the left of the decimal point, beginning with the general overall classification and major subdivisions; for example, numbers from 900–999 refer to an overall classification which includes Biography, Geography and History. English History, for instance, is 940. To the right of the decimal point come the smaller subdivisions. These get more and more specific the further you move to the right.

The Dewey system has been used successfully for over a hundred years because it can handle an almost infinite number of subdivisions and therefore has adapted to the explosion of information available.

Most libraries are laid out so that the books come in the same order as they do in the Dewey system. However, as there are always exceptions you should familiarize yourself thoroughly with the libraries you use and know where to find useful extras such as shelves full of oversized books that cannot be kept with the rest of their classification.

The reference library

Familiarize yourself with what is available. You will probably be amazed at the subject reference books, journals, bibliographies (lists of books on specific subjects) and catalogues (such as those of books kept in other major libraries) that are available and that you probably never dreamed existed.

Repeated leisurely visits to the library will help you add an extra dimension and interest to all your work.

9

Making Notes and Taking Notes

When you understand clearly what your notes are for you will be half way to making a better job of them. They are *not* a sort of ritual you have to go through but never refer to again. They are *not* a way of reproducing, in as much detail as possible, the lecture you have heard or the book you have read.

Your notes should be a *clear, basic outline* of the facts you need to know. Use them as:

(a) basic information for exam revision;
(b) a framework to support additional information as you come across it;
(c) a trigger, to remind you of all the other information you have come across and to help it settle into place.

You can *make* your own notes from books or you can *take* notes from teachers, lecturers or educational programmes.

Making notes

Since you want your notes to work as hard as possible for you make them as clear as possible. Ideally you should be able to make sense of them months after you have written them.

Making your own notes, rather than taking them from dictation, makes them easier for you to learn because they reflect your own way of thinking and remembering.

1. Use a loose-leaf system

This will make it easy to add to notes and rearrange them. A ring binder is probably the best; papers in envelope files and box files can get out of order.

2. *Leave space for changes and additions*

Work from one basic textbook or set of lecture notes to compile the first framework of notes but leave plenty of space for later changes and additions.

- Write on *one side* of the paper only so that the reverse side can be used for comments/additions to the facing page.
- Leave *generous spaces* between the lines and *wide margins* on either side for additions and alterations.

3. *Note your sources*

You may wish to refer again later to a book you have used for reference; if you have kept the details it will save a lot of time and trouble.

- Write the title, author, library reference number and where the book is kept at the top of the notes.
- Note chapter and page numbers in the margin next to the notes you have made from them, then you can quickly refer to the information again.
- Keep a list with your notes of *all* the books you have read on the subject, even if they have not been used for notes. One useful method of doing this is to list the books under the title of the essay or project for which they were consulted.

4. *Find a pattern of information*

Understanding and learning notes will be much easier if you can see a recognizable pattern and logical sequence through the facts. Try and identify this pattern *before* you start making a set of notes.

- The writer or lecturer will have assembled the facts according to a plan or method.
- Try to identify the author's plan (like x-raying the skeleton inside the body); use it to form a basic, logical structure for your own notes. You will do this much more easily if you read

quickly through the information and give yourself time to think about it before you start to make notes (see Chapter 8 on effective reading).

5. Aim for clarity

● Keep notes simple.
● Use single words or short phrases *not* full sentences and paragraphs.
● Give definitions of new terms and words when they are introduced.
● Use a variety of mathematical and shorthand symbols to save time and space. Useful examples include: e.g. (for example), i.e. (that is) ‹ (leads to/resulted in/greater than), ∴ (therefore), ∵ (because), + (with), NB (note well). You can develop your own shorthand for words that crop up a lot in your own subject. For example, names can be referred to by initial letters only.

6. Break down notes into sections

You will not be able to remember easily a mass of undigestible facts presented in prose. Write the notes so that they make a clear and easily memorized pattern on the page.

● Use the original pattern if possible (see note 4).
● Think in terms of cause and effect. Isolate the major points and make sure you have noted:

(a) the reasons that led up to them or caused them;
(b) the results that stemmed from them or the arguments they prove.

By constantly asking yourself questions such as 'What is the main point? Why did it happen? What happened as a result? What does it prove? Who caused this or influenced it?' you will make notes that fundamentally make sense and that are broken down into logical sections. This will help you answer similar questions when they appear in exams.

Never make notes without thinking. They will be little use to you when you come to revise.

- Devise your own regular pattern for presenting notes so that you can easily distinguish between major sections and minor points of information.
- Give yourself short, clear points to remember by dividing and subdividing the major headings, for example:

MAJOR SECTIONS IN CAPITAL LETTERS UNDER-LINED

(B) IF THERE ARE MANY SECTIONS DISTINGUISH THEM BY LETTERS OF THE ALPHABET

USE CAPITAL LETTERS FOR MAIN HEADINGS

(c) Use letters of the alphabet to list important points.

1. Numbers can be used to split up minor points of information.

1.i And Roman numerals can break the information up still further

1.ii Yet still show that the facts are related to the same overall topic.

- Marker pens and coloured pens can usefully highlight important areas.
- You will devise a system that suits you through trial and error.

Some subjects or topics will divide up more neatly than others but if you keep the main framework clear and points short you will have a much easier scheme to re-read and remember than if you write out notes in continuous prose.

7. Include examples

- Include examples of what you refer to; these should be learned by heart so that they can be used in exams.
- Include short quotations from original sources or respected

authorities. Learn these by heart – they make a good impression in exams.

8. Keep refining your notes

It is unlikely that one set of notes from one book will be adequate on its own. You should go back to them and rework them when you have new information to add.

- Rearranging your notes and making them as logical as possible is an important part of the learning/revising process.
- If you have left sufficient space in your original notes you should be able to add to them without making them illegible and messy.
- As part of getting your notes in a good, logical order file your essays immediately after the notes on which they are based. They can then be read straight after the notes as part of revision.
- If notes become too messy with additions then take time out to rewrite them and tidy them up.
- If rewriting use the opportunity to improve on the organization of the notes, in the light of what you have learned since you first made them. This will not be a waste of time because it will help you memorize the notes, and also help you improve their structure so that they become easier to memorize.
- Constantly refining your notes is an important part of the learning process.

Taking notes

Everything you have learned about making notes applies equally to taking notes.

1. Listen effectively

- Instead of reading effectively to see the structure and purpose of a textbook you will have to listen effectively to recognize the logical development and purpose of the lecture or notes that are being dictated. To listen effectively you have to:

(a) look for the logical structure in what is being said;
(b) keep questioning in your mind everything the speaker says;
(c) look for causes and effects;
(d) concentrate.

2. Fill in gaps later

- If you think you have missed something leave a very obvious gap as a reminder; carry on and return to it when the lesson/ lecture is over. If the teacher is unavailable to fill you in on the missing information ask a fellow student.

3. Rewrite notes

It is almost impossible to take down fully adequate notes as you hear them. Rewrite them as soon as possible, imposing a clearer structure on them. This rewriting will also help you learn the information.

10

Essays and Written Work

Essays form a part of most exams and are unavoidable in study. You must learn to write adequate essays in order to succeed.

Examination essays are used to assess how much you know and whether you can analyse and convey that knowledge. Study essays help you consolidate what you know. They also test whether or not you really understand what you have learned. It may be helpful to view essay writing as trying to explain to a friend what you have learned, in a clear, logical way.

Do not use the fact that you are not a brilliant writer as an excuse for poor marks in essay questions. Bad marks for essays are rarely caused by lack of literary talent, but more usually by basic failings that can be put right.

As with any skill, writing, including essay writing, will improve with practice. The more trouble you take to write clear, concise and thoughtful essays when there is no pressure the easier it will be to write fluently and logically under examination conditions.

The most common reasons for doing badly in essay questions are:

(a) *Not answering the actual question which has been asked.*

Put so bluntly this seems rather unlikely. However, it happens all too easily, especially when people are panicking, rushing to write before they have had time to think or latching on to a few key words in the question and assuming they know what it is all about.

(b) *No coherent and logical theme or 'point' to the essay.*

The question needs an answer (a conclusion). Just rambling on about facts and ideas vaguely related to the essay topic will result in poor marks, however much you write.

(c) *Poor presentation, handwriting, spelling and grammar.*

Try to break away from the idea that clear handwriting and correct grammar and spelling are only incidentals. Think of them as the basic toolkit you need to communicate your ideas clearly. Do not let yourself down by neglecting them.

If you recognize any of these three as the reasons you are doing badly in essay questions you will be encouraged to know that there are some straightforward steps you can take that will result in immediate improvement.

Basic steps in essay writing

1. *'Apply the seat of the pants to the seat of the chair'*

This was the answer given by Mark Twain, American author of *Huckleberry Finn* and other literary classics, when asked the secret of being a writer.

It is very easy to put off writing an essay, especially if you feel that you are not good at it. Actually sitting down and deciding to get the essay finished within a certain space of time is the best possible cure for a writing 'block'.

Try and tackle essays at the time of day when you work best.

2. *Read and understand the question*

You *must* give yourself time to think about the question rather than rushing into an answer. Given adequate time to think things through, your brain will have the chance to work like the brilliant computer it is, making associations and drawing conclusions almost of its own accord.

Read the question

- Look closely at the question before you start on the answer. Take time to do this, even in examination conditions.
- Ask some questions, even saying them out loud if you are on your own. The answers will give you a much clearer picture of what the questioner is wanting to find out.

- Here are a few basic questions to get you started every time.

    (a) What general theme is the questioner asking about?
    (b) What particular answer is the questioner trying to find out?
    (c) What facts do I know which are relevant to the general theme and the particular topic?
    (d) Does the question ask for illustration in the form of graphs, drawings, maps etc.?

Understand the question

- Underline the key words and phrases that occur in the question. Write your answer according to the instructions they give.
- You *must* understand the meanings of the key words which crop up time and again in essay questions.

Common words and phrases are:

Word	Meaning
Briefly	Concisely, without unnecessary elaboration
Cause	The reason or motive for a particular result
Compare	How great are the similarities between . . . (in the answer refer also to the differences)
Contrast	Show the differences between . . . (you should also refer to the similarities)
Compare and Contrast	Show the similarities and differences between . . . Draw a conclusion about whether the differences are greater than the similarities
Criticize	Assess and pass judgment on . . . giving your reasons and evidence to support your opinions. NB: In this context the word criticize does not mean take a negative view. Your conclusion could be either positive or negative.

Define	Give the precise meaning of the word or phrase in this particular context, with reference to any other possible interpretations . . .
Demonstrate	Describe and explain with the help of experiments that . . . *or* Prove the truth of . . . (the proposition or argument)
Describe	Give the characteristics of . . . Give a word picture of . . .
Discuss	State all the conflicting sides of the argument before deciding which one, if any, is correct or which one has the greatest weight of argument on its side
Evaluate	Estimate the value or amount of . . . (the proposition or idea); give your own conclusion
Explain	Make clear the cause, origin or meaning of . . . *or* Interpret the meaning of . . .
Illustrate	Explain/demonstrate/make clear an idea or statement by the use of diagrams . . . *or* Back up an argument by giving clear examples (such as quotations)
Justify	Show the correctness of a particular statement/ argument by giving adequate reasons for it
Outline	Give a summary of the essential points of . . .
Summarize	State briefly the main facts of . . . without giving detailed information; sum up

There will be other key words which you know crop up frequently in the particular subjects you are studying. If you do not understand their meaning find out what they mean *right now*. Ask a teacher or look up the words in the dictionary, or ask fellow students what they think. You should not allow yourself to continue while you are feeling unsure of basic vocabulary.

3. Make a plan and use it

Never begin an essay from now on without making a well-constructed plan first. You need for every essay a plan which:

- assesses the question clearly;
- looks at the arguments involved;
- backs up opinions and statements with facts;
- comes to a conclusion that states your answer to the question.

A typical basic plan will consist of introduction, development of the theme, and conclusion.

Introduction

You need one paragraph giving a brief resumé of the question and your approach to it but without going into the details. *Quotations* are often useful ingredients in introductory paragraphs. They attract attention and you can agree or disagree with them as a way of getting into the main theme, for example, take the essay title: 'Winston has been described as the only fully developed character in George Orwell's novel *1984*. Do you agree with this view and if so does it constitute a weakness in the novel?'

This question is about whether *1984* is a vehicle for conveying political beliefs rather than what actually happens to the characters. An amusing way of getting into the essay might be:

It has been said of George Orwell that he would not blow his nose without moralizing on conditions in the handkerchief industry . . .

This shows you have understood the point of the question and gets the essay off to a lively start. You may have come across this quotation during your study of the set text, especially if you have found time to read around the subject and learn a little about

George Orwell himself. However, you do not have to be a great genius or amazingly widely read to use this technique. Simply use one of the dictionaries of quotations readily available to you in any good library. There are many collections of quotations which you can look at to find suitable quotations for a wide range of essays (see Useful Information, p. 95).

Here is another example. Take the essay title: 'Why did Britain lose the American War of Independence?'

You know George Washington was one of the most important American leaders. Look him up in a Dictionary of Quotations and you have a good chance of finding one of his comments which will get you into the essay, for example:

George Washington, on being given command of the rebel American forces in 1775 said 'I can answer but for three things, a firm belief in the justice of our cause, close attention in the prosecution of it, and the strictest integrity.' His words give an insight into some of the fundamental reasons why the Americans were able to overcome the British . . .

Not only does this make a good, positive start to the essay, it may also help to trigger a few ideas in your mind about how to approach the essay. Of course you cannot do this for every essay as your technique would become rather obvious. Similarly, not every subject or essay question lends itself to doing so. But subjects such as literature, history and economics, which are strongly based around people and their ideas, are ideally suited to the use of quotations.

This method is really for use during term time when you have time to think around your essays and project work and when looking for quotations will help extend your working knowledge of the libraries and introduce you to a wide range of available sources.

However, for literature exams you will be expected to learn quotations from set texts. It would also be well worth the trouble of learning a few key quotations for other subjects so that you have them at your fingertips when you are in the exam room.

They do not have to be long. Just make sure that every quotation you use, wherever it comes in your essay or project, is there to make a point.

Development of the theme in several linking paragraphs

For example, paragraph 2 might be background information necessary for understanding the context of the question; paragraph 3, arguments for the proposition, with examples; and paragraph 4, arguments against the proposition, with examples.

Conclusion

Here you need one paragraph in which you answer the question, summarizing your reasons.

To get your plan into some sort of order, like that shown above, first write down briefly, preferably using single words or short phrases, all the facts and information you think you will need to answer the question. Try to assemble the words and phrases in roughly the right order as you go along. To make this possible leave plenty of spaces between lines and in the margins for later additions and changes and reminders. Add reminders/notes of where you need examples, quotations, statistics, diagrams etc. to back up your statements.

Write a brief phase or two to indicate the line of your introduction, and the same to summarize your conclusion. Make sure that everything you write builds towards that conclusion.

You are unlikely to have made a perfect plan which does not need alterations. But unless you have got into a real muddle you do not need to rewrite the plan. Give numbers to your basic paragraphs. Then go through the plan and put matching numbers next to all the facts that have to be in a particular paragraph. For example, mark with a 1. all the facts, ideas, quotations etc. that you intend to include in the introduction.

Double-check that you have not included a lot of irrelevant information. Refer to the plan constantly as you write the essay. It is meant to be *used* not just as a sort of good-luck ritual. Check at the end of every paragraph or section (you may need to develop more than one paragraph on a particular theme) that you have included everything you intended to include.

Remember:

- You cannot write a good essay without a proper plan.
- Planning soon gets easier with practice.

4. Prepare a first draft

This will not always be necessary. There will not be time to do a complete draft in exam conditions so you should work towards finding it comfortable as soon as possible to go directly from a good, detailed plan to writing the final essay.

However, if you lack confidence about essays it is probably best to begin by writing draft versions on rough paper before you do the final versions. When you do a draft read it through as though you were marking it. Does it answer the question? Is everything relevant to the question and not unnecessary waffle? Does it make use of the facts to show the arguments? Is it legible? Are punctuation and grammar accurate? Is there a clear and logical conclusion?

5. Write readable, effective essays

- Be concise rather than wordy.
- Keep sentences simple.
- Avoid slang and colloquial expressions.
- Avoid clichés and 'overworked' words like nice, strong, good, etc. which have lost their impact.
- Ensure that separate points, themes and concepts are dealt with in separate paragraphs.
- Give a logical structure to paragraphs as well as longer pieces of work; for example, if giving historical examples make sure they come in chronological order. Do not dodge about within the paragraph.
- If you need to break a paragraph to prevent it becoming overlong and unwieldy, make the break at a logical point.
- *Always* give examples and reasons to back up your statements or they will look like meaningless waffle.

- Come to a conclusion. This is the answer to the question. If you do not give a conclusion you have failed in your fundamental task – to answer the question that has been put to you.

6. Pay attention to good presentation

Don't let carelessness spoil a good essay.

Handwriting

If your handwriting is hard to read the examiner will inevitably feel irritated. Marks will be lost if relevant facts cannot be deciphered. In the worst cases examiners have refused altogether to mark badly written examination papers.

- Do not start from scratch to learn a new script, especially if you have a lot of other things to learn at the same time. Instead make a conscious effort to improve the handwriting you already use. Over a period of time you can change your bad habits simply by repeating better ones.
- Is your handwriting too small and cramped? Try to make it larger, putting more space into your letters. You may find that your hand is cramped rather hard around the pen. If you can relax your hand more your handwriting will open out.
- Are some letters illegible or confusing? Look at your writing, or better still get someone else to look at it, and note the letters and combinations of letters that are causing most confusion.

  Practise just a few minutes every day writing those particular letters out in a really perfect 'textbook' sort of way and then try and remember to do this when you are writing normally.
- Is your writing slow? Does it hold you up in exams? The most common cause of slow writing is taking the pen up from the paper after forming the letters. Make a point of keeping your pen on the page all the time. Do not lift it off except to add dots or crosses to letters. It will be hard at first but you will be pleased when you see your new, faster, flowing handwriting.

- Ballpoint pens are particularly difficult to write with well. You will do yourself greater justice with a fountain pen or a felt-tip or similar pen which writes more like a fountain pen.

Spelling, grammar and punctuation

If these three present problems do not ignore them and hope they will go away.

- There are basic rules which can be learned and lists of the exceptions. Several books with a straightforward, adult approach to helping with spelling and grammar are listed at the end of this book (p. 94).
- Use easy learning techniques, for example mnemonics such as 'i before e except after c' or keeping cards with troublesome words on, which can be looked at in spare moments.
- Get friends to test you.

Logical sequence

It is important to keep to a logical sequence within sentences and paragraphs as well as within the overall development of the essay. A logical development of your argument will impress teachers and examiners even if they disagree with your conclusions.

Projects and extended course-work

Projects and extended course-work are now a major element of study and an integral part of many end-of-course examinations. The trend is to combine a timed, written examination with an assessment of projects done during the term. An overall assessment of work done during the term may also be taken into account.

It is no longer sufficient to jog along during the year and then try and pull out all the stops for the short period of the examinations. Now more than ever before students are well advised to keep up a steady pace of work throughout their course.

All the good habits you have learned so far will contribute to making your projects and extended course-work more successful. Basic advice about being organized, planning and presenting written work as effectively as possible, matter more than ever with project work because you have to rely on yourself and use your own initiative.

In addition to all the demands made by more conventional exam methods you also need to work on an additional skill – finding material and making use of all available resources.

There is one major plus about projects and extended course-work: you do not have to show what you can do in the short space of a timed examination. With careful planning you can take the panic out of this aspect of the exam. Projects are a major bonus to people who find that nerves prevent them from doing their best in examination conditions.

If you develop a systematic method for tackling projects and follow it step by step you will save time and avoid the major pitfall of this type of work – treating each project as a totally separate entity, without benefiting from what you have learned from previous projects.

The following is a good basic plan of action. As you gain more experience you can adapt it to suit your own working methods.

1. Find the right topic

Your teacher will set the basic theme but may well give you some choice as to how you actually approach it. At GCSE level you may have very little choice about this. You will probably be given a fairly narrow range of topics or set of guidelines by your teacher, who will know what needs to be covered to give the best chance in the exam.

At college or university you may feel you have almost too much choice. In effect you will probably be asked to provide your own extended essay title within a very general theme. The challenge will be to choose something which allows you to demonstrate what you are able to do. The advantage is that you can angle it to emphasize those aspects of the subject that you like best.

If the topic is general you must first narrow it down to a specific title. Take care with this stage. You should aim for a title with which you can cope in the time available, one on which you can find plenty of information and one which is adapted to your own particular interests and way of working.

- Get a blank piece of paper, look at the information you have been given and start asking questions about it. Try all the options: When? Where? Who? How? Why? Which? How much? Write down all the ideas and thoughts that come in answer to these basic questions and any others that occur to you. Make a determined effort to think as widely and as imaginatively as possible.
- What emerges?

  Perhaps you have been given the general topic: 'Scientific discovery in the nineteenth century.' If you are interested in people and their lives more than scientific facts you may find you want to look at this through the lives and achievements of one or two selected scientists such as Louis Pasteur and Mendel.

  If you are more interested in theories and ideas you may like to approach the subject by asking how much do twentieth century advances owe to nineteenth century scientists.
- If you have been given one person as a topic do not just settle for a simple chronology of their life. Ask questions again and devise a title which puts the person in a context. If you take, for example, Florence Nightingale – do not just write her story from birth to death. Try to show the importance of her life by setting yourself a title with the question in it such as: 'What was Florence Nightingale's contribution to the development of nursing?' or 'Florence Nightingale was a pioneer in her time. How relevant are her ideas today?'
- When you have a title that you think will work check it with your teacher or supervisor before you go ahead. Teachers cannot give you specific help with projects but they can advise you.

2. Locate sources of information

When you have finalized the title for your project or extended essay make an exhaustive list of all possible sources of information. These may include:

- Libraries
- Foreign embassies, tourist offices and trade centres
- Museums and art galleries
- Cathedrals, castles, stately homes or National Trust properties
- Trade unions
- Guilds and livery companies in the City of London
- Associations and trade groups, such as the Design Council
- Big companies with press and information departments, such as British Steel
- Individuals with relevant knowledge or experience, for example grandparents for information about the war years, parish clergy about the history of the local church, local doctors about health in your area, etc.
- Local history societies (through local libraries)
- Charities and pressure groups, such as the British Heart Foundation or the Sports Council
- Old newspapers (available on microfilm at some large libraries)
- Visits to locations to familiarize yourself with the subject and to get local material, guide books etc. (take a taperecorder to note your reactions and observations and to get interviews from people such as cathedral guides)

Try to think of other sources of information. Discuss possibilities with teachers, friends and relatives.

Libraries

These are the first resource for almost any project.

The person who sets the project may also give you a *bibliography*, a list of books where you will find relevant information. If you are not given a starter bibliography go straight to the catalogue in the library. Look up the key words in the project title. List the names of the appropriate books to make your new bibliography and make a note of the Dewey numbers (see p. 44) of the key words so that you can look for other books under the same number in different libraries.

Do not forget to look in general reference books such as *The Encyclopaedia Britannica.*

Look at the list of contents and in the index to see if a book has information which is relevant.

Libraries are excellent sources of information on local topics such as local history or trades. If the librarian is helpful, ask for advice. Most librarians are very helpful. Keep their goodwill by doing as much as you can yourself and not wasting time on unnecessary queries.

Make sure the reference books you use are as up to date as possible.

Organizations

You can use the business and services phone book for the London area to locate a lot of these addresses. There should be a copy in your local reference library. You will also find a wide range of other useful trade directories and reference books.

Town halls and libraries are a good source of information about local firms and places of interest that you cannot get to yourself. If possible telephone first and ask if there is any charge before sending for leaflets and other material. When writing for information keep your letter brief, clear and to the point. Explain you are doing a project/dissertation and that you would appreciate any help the organization might be able to give. Remember to send a large, self-addressed stamped envelope when asking for information.

Newspapers

Old newspapers can provide a lot of useful information for certain types of project. As well as looking in libraries try local newspaper offices and older relatives and friends who may have kept copies of particularly interesting newspapers.

3. Organize your project

When you have decided on your topic and worked out from where the information is most likely to come you must organize a plan of campaign for your project. It will have to be integrated into your timetable. As project work has become an important part of many courses you may find you have to deal with more than one project at the same time, so good organization is vital.

Start a project file

A card index system is probably most flexible (see p. 28); or you may prefer a shorthand notebook. Keep separate files for each project.

- Make a note of everything that has to be done: who to telephone, write to, which libraries to visit, which individuals to speak to, etc. Note the date on which you did things and make a note of when replies/information are expected back.
- Slot the project into your timetable. As soon as you have a fairly clear idea of the amount of time involved rework your timetable to take in project work. Note time set aside for project work, including library visits, discussions with teachers, visits to individuals for interviews, etc. in your diary. Make sure the project work can be completed comfortably in the time you have allocated.
- Send off for information straight away. You will have a limited time to complete the project so you cannot waste time getting the information together. This is particularly the case where you may have to wait to receive information back. As soon as you have located sources write letters or telephone straight away. You can be getting on with other things while waiting for information to come back.

4. Plan/design

Just as with an essay your project should be put together according to a well thought-through plan. In addition it will need a design to take into account illustrations and diagrams. Properly planned and designed your project/dissertation should be presented as a fully comprehensive and well-documented report on the topic you were given.

- When you have the basic ideas and have marshalled resources plan sections/chapters in the same way as planning an essay (see p. 56) – keep to a logical format, not just within the overall project but within the separate sections; do a few pages in a draft version to begin with. This will help you find the style, tone and level of information you will be working to. Do as much as you can in draft so that the final version looks as professional as possible.
- Use a looseleaf system for writing up, so that you can add to it, correct mistakes or change pages without ruining the entire project.
- Include a contents page to go at the front.
- List your sources at the end, including your own bibliography.
- Create a good, strong front page with the title, your name, the date and any other relevant information.

5. Use illustrations and diagrams

Unless you are specifically told not to you should use well-chosen illustrative material, diagrams, maps, charts, etc. to illustrate your project.

Sources

- Try and use your imagination when looking for illustrations just as you should when researching the information.
- Specialist museums are an excellent source of postcards and other illustrations (see p. 96, Useful Information). If you cannot get there yourself (maybe it is too far away) it is a good idea to phone up and ask if they will sell you postcards or a brochure by post. As well as using obvious sources like museums take another look at the list of resources you have drawn up. Could they be used as a source of illustration as well as information?

Handy hints

A good tip when buying highly illustrated brochures is to get two rather than one. Otherwise you will always find that the two pictures you most want to use are back to back on the same page and you cannot use both!

You can now get excellent quality colour photocopies. So if you have old books that cannot be cut up or which do not belong to you, copies of the illustrations can still be used for your project.

Children's reference books are often more highly illustrated than adult books. Market stalls and junk shops often have old magazines or postcards that may be useful to you.

If your school/college has word-processors or desk-top publishing try to use them for at least part of the project. They can be especially useful for creating charts and diagrams.

Using illustrations

Give illustrations accurate captions. It is not enough just to paste in the pictures. They must be integrated properly into the text.

State the source of illustrations, giving dates where appropriate. Indicate why the illustration has been chosen. For example, you could illustrate a project on the history of the bicycle with a picture of an early bicycle, taken from a magazine of the time. An uninspired caption might read: 'An early bicycle, known as a 'boneshaker' ''. However you would gain far more marks if you wrote a fuller caption such as:

> This is a humorous cartoon from an early edition of *Punch* magazine, published in 1867. At this time the bicycle was known as a 'boneshaker' because of its wooden wheels. The cartoon demonstrates the painful accuracy of the name and shows that these vehicles were regarded as rather absurd when they first appeared.

6. Make it individual

To get the best marks for a project/dissertation you need to make it stand out from the crowd (for the right reasons of course!).

One way in which it can do this is by being immaculately planned and presented. Although that means a lot of work you will be surprised how much more satisfaction you will get than if you just throw something together in a short time.

The other way in which you can make your work stand out is by introducing that extra special element that says that you have done something more than just the basic work expected.

Try and find ways of enlivening what might be a rather tedious subject. Here are some ideas, but try and think of some of your own.

- Use humorous (but apt) quotations.
- Make at least part of your project about individuals; this will automatically make it more interesting than a general thesis, rather as a photograph is always more interesting if there is a person in it.
- Try to find people who can add personal experiences and reminiscences to what you have to say, so that the subject comes alive.
- Inject a personal element where appropriate, by using your own relatives' experience, or pinpointing an area you know well or an unusual place that you have visited as a focal point for part of the project.
- Take your own photographs or make your own drawings instead of using existing illustrations only.

11

Revision Techniques

1. Start in good time

Panicking because you have left things to the last minute makes concentration difficult.

2. Check the syllabus

Make sure you know what is on the syllabus. Check with your teacher or in the syllabus published by the examining board (addresses are given at the end of this book).

3. Check the 'core' topics

These are the compulsory sections of the exam. Make sure you know what they are. If necessary look at the syllabus.

Core topics must take priority in your revision scheme.

4. Make a revision timetable

- This should be drawn up like a study timetable.
- Look at the total available time before the exams, allocate a part of it to each subject.
- Divide the days into sections of 30–45 minutes and allocate them to the various subjects making sure that there is the right total time for each subject.
- Make lists of what has to be covered in each section allocated to each topic. As you finish each topic cross it off.
- Alternate between the various subjects so that you do not get bored by too long on one topic.
- Plan to begin each revision session with a favourite subject so that it's easier to get started.
- Take regular short breaks.
- Leave adequate time for meals and exercise/fresh air.

5. Get actively involved in revision

Like any learning process revision will be most successful if you get actively involved rather than just re-reading notes (see Chapter 7 on learning and remembering).

Try the following methods and devise other 'active' forms of revision for all your topics.

- Summarize each topic when you think you know it.
- Make charts and diagrams to illustrate theories or sequences of events.
- Devise tests for yourself. Use a computer for this if you have access to one.
- Discuss work with other people.
- Make lists of possible questions. Write answers to some of them.
- Make lists of quotations/formulae/vocabulary/dates/etc. and learn them.

6. Practise timed exam papers

This will make you familiar with the papers and help you get experience of planning and timing questions.

7. Form a partnership

If possible find someone else whose workload is similar to yours. You can help reinforce each other's willpower when your spirits are sagging!

- Test each other on what you have learned. This will help both of you to learn better.
- Talk over what you are learning. Exchanging ideas is a useful part of the learning process.

8. Use a tape recorder

- Use tape recorders for practising vocabulary or listening to facts which have to be learned by repetition.
- If you have oral examinations get used to saying answers out loud so that you do not feel embarrassed by speaking out in an exam situation.

9. Use the library

- You should have become familiar with your library and all the services it has to offer by the time you come to take major exams.
- Among the useful reference books kept by the library will be study aids and books with 'shortcuts' to the answers needed for exams.

These are no substitute for a really thorough knowledge and understanding of the subject, but they can be a useful extra when it comes to polishing up information specifically for exams.

Some useful titles are listed at the end of this book (p. 94).

10. Go into training

If you are at your best physically you will do better in examinations.

- Sensible rest, relaxation, exercise and eating, will help you make the most of thorough groundwork (see Chapter 15 on controlling stress and anxiety).
- Get into training for the exam schedule. If this means changing your times of getting up in the morning and going to bed then the sooner you make a new habit of this the better.

  Start getting up about an hour before you need to leave the house to get to the exam room on time without rushing. Start going to bed at an hour which means you can get up at the right time without feeling terrible!

11. Look beyond the exams

Plan something good for afterwards to help you keep a sense of proportion.

Exam revision don'ts

1. Don't panic.
2. Don't leave new learning until it is time to 'revise'.
3. Don't get overtired.

4. Don't forget to take time off.
5. Don't revise right up until bedtime. Stop and do something to relax or your brain will be too overstimulated for you to sleep properly.
6. Don't associate with people who make you depressed or anxious.
7. Don't drink too much coffee.
8. Don't use drugs (pills or alcohol) to help you get through, even if other people recommend them.

12

Coping with Anxiety and Stress

Anxiety prevents concentration, this stops you from working effectively, which creates more anxiety and gets you into a vicious circle.

Of course you should be keyed up for an exam. If you were too laid back you probably would not do your best. But if you are experiencing any of these symptoms – crying for no good reason, sleeplessness, studying long hours without anything seeming to stick, withdrawn silences, erratic eating patterns – then you are feeling more stressed than you should.

The advice given in this chapter is sometimes called stress management. Much of it is plain commonsense.

You have to make a *positive decision* that you want to eliminate as much stress from your life as possible. Approach coping with anxiety in a methodical way, just like learning to do anything else.

Remember too that advice on how to work towards exams is there to help you. Use just as much of it as you personally find useful, without following it slavishly. Do not let it become another source of anxiety because you are not following advice absolutely to the letter.

Eliminating causes of anxiety

1. Break the anxiety circle

Make sure you are following the basic advice given so far. This will give you the confidence that you are approaching things the right way.

2. Check you are happy with your overall goal

If you are happy that you are making progress in your plans for the future you will not feel anxious that you are wasting time.

3. Keep studies and daily life organized

Good organization, which you know you can rely on, will cut out the strain of having to keep lots of details in your head.

- Write everything down.
- Make timetables.
- Keep lists.

4. Keep notes/references clearly filed

Muddle is very stress-inducing. Sorting out muddled paperwork helps you get your thoughts organized and boosts confidence.

5. Prioritize

Stop and take time to think, however overstressed and anxious you are. Work out what is really important and what can wait until later.

- When time is limited make sure that only really important tasks are given priority. Let the rest wait.
- At very busy times ignore some jobs altogether while you concentrate on your studies and getting through the exams. Don't feel guilty about it. You are doing the right thing. Nobody will know or remember if your meals were home-made, your hair curled, your lawn cut or your bicycle cleaned.
- Don't let unimportant tasks become an excuse for not getting on with what really matters.

6. Use time sensibly

- Use time saving methods such as fast reading techniques.
- Do not waste time on aimless worrying. If you cannot concentrate on a major task at least use the time to get something useful out of the way such as making your lists or sorting your notes.

- If you think you will not be able to complete something on time, such as an essay, worrying will only make it harder to concentrate. Bite the bullet and speak to the teacher or whoever is expecting you to have done the work. *Reschedule* it sensibly so that you have sufficient time to do the work with a troublefree mind.

7. Always check instructions

Getting things right first time saves time wasted on redoing things.

Anti-stress techniques

1. Eat properly

Study and examinations are demanding. They need a healthy approach to living, just like any other major endeavour.

- Eat regularly and eat proper food. There are plenty of books available to advise you on a sensible diet.
- Snacking on junk food and sweets will confuse your body and make it less efficient.

2. Take exercise

If you think regular exercise is only important to people involved with very physical tasks you might be interested to know that top chess players train physically as well as mentally for big matches. Exercise does two important things:

- It uses up the adrenaline that is making you anxious. A good bout of exercise will help to calm you down if you are feeling het up.
- It keeps your body healthy and able to respond better to heavy work schedules and exams. If your body is not fit your brain will not function at top efficiency.

If you do not like games or sports try to take a good walk at least three times a week.

3. Get enough fresh air

Your body needs oxygen. You cannot work at peak efficiency if you stay for hours in a poorly ventilated room.

4. Get enough sleep

Tiredness adds to anxiety. It makes you work less effectively. There is nothing noble about working through the night.

- If anxiety is keeping you awake respond by getting organized so that you know you have thought of everything and do not need to worry unnecessarily.
- Keep a notebook and pen by your bed. If you wake in the night worrying about things you must do *write them down*. This way you can be sure you will not forget them in the morning and you will find it easier to relax.

5. Avoid caffeine

A quick shot of caffeine from time to time can work wonders when you need an extra boost. However, too much caffeine can create the exact symptoms of anxiety and stress.

- If you drink a lot of coffee 'to keep you going' you may find that the anxiety you think you are feeling because of impending exams is really brought about by the coffee you are drinking while you study.
- Caffeine stops you sleeping properly. Like anxiety it causes you to wake after a few hours. Find out how much of your anxiety is actually a reaction to caffeine by cutting out strong coffee and chocolate for a few days and seeing how you feel.
- If you cannot manage to study without a steaming mug of something by your side try an alternative such as decaffeinated coffee, tea (although this also has quite a lot of caffeine), hot milk, fruit juice, etc.
- If your body has come to depend on caffeine then try to break

yourself of the habit over a period of days by gradually mixing decaffeinated and ordinary coffee until you are using just decaffeinated.

- Caffeine also makes you want to go to the loo, which could be a problem in the exam!

6. Talk to someone

Worries get put into perspective and anxiety and stress are reduced if you can talk things over and literally get them out of your system.

- If you have a study partner as has been suggested then you are obviously doing a certain amount of this already. If not, talk to friends and family or teachers and tutors.
- Some colleges and schools have counsellors specifically to help students with their worries and problems. Make use of them if you need to discuss anxieties. Obviously they have all been through the exam hurdles to get where they are so their approach will be sympathetic.

7. Accept yourself

If you are finding that all your efforts to overcome anxiety are not succeeding then as a last resort (not in a moment of panic) question whether you have taken on too much. It may be better to shed some of your workload and do well at what is left.

- This is not something to be decided without talking it over with your teacher or someone whose opinion you value. You can probably manage simply to *reschedule* some of the work and take the exams at different times.
- If, after sensible discussion, you find rescheduling your workload is the answer do not allow this to depress you. Keep away from the trap of comparing yourself with other people. People have different capacities for taking exams just like everything else.

Start your new schedule in a positive frame of mind and

congratulate yourself for having the sense to organize things in a way which suits you.

8. Learn to relax

There are plenty of books on how to achieve relaxation. Basic relaxation courses, either in books, classes or on tape, show you how to switch your mind off from day-to-day anxieties and how to let your body go limp a little at a time until you are completely relaxed.

- A relaxation tape is a good way of learning to relax because it brings in someone else who tells you what to do. Tapes can usually be bought at health shops or your doctor may be able to recommend one.
- Monitor yourself from time to time. Are your teeth clenched, is the back of your neck stiff, are your knees tense, is your spine rigid? Consciously go through these areas one by one and relax them. Smile to yourself and feel your facial muscles soften. Do this as often as you remember and you will help prevent a build-up of tension.
- Relaxation techniques have to be practised regularly to become totally effective. Try them before you go to sleep or when you feel particularly edgy.

9. Look beyond the exams

However important exams may seem there *is* a life beyond them, whatever the outcome.

- Although this book aims to improve study and exam results it does not mean that you have to get these aims out of proportion. Many successful people, from Winston Churchill to Richard Branson, have been bad at exams.
- Plan something to look forward to after the exams. This is not self-indulgence, but an important part of approaching exams in the right frame of mind.

Staying calm

Here are some techniques for preventing last-minute nerves from taking over.

1. Do not panic

Panic can be almost comforting. It allows you the option of giving up and running away. When you feel panic coming on decide *not to panic*. Making that decision is half the battle.

2. Breathe deeply

A minute or so of deep breaths, taken at a regular pace, will help your body to calm down. It's a cliché but it works.

3. Take your time

Make a conscious decision not to rush into doing anything, especially writing the answers to an exam. Give yourself a few moments to think while you take those deep breaths.

4. Practise relaxation

Pinpoint where the tension is concentrated in your body and consciously relax those muscles.

5. Get things in perspective

Do not allow minor hurdles to panic you. Always keep the long-term aims in view. As long as you are making some progress towards those a momentary lapse will not be the end of the world.

6. Avoid comparisons

- Get on with your own life without constantly comparing your achievements to someone else's.
- Have confidence in your own individual abilities and approach to what you are doing.
- Do not allow others to shake your calm.
- Ignore the sort of people who tell you how much they have done, who start panic rumours, who appear to write non-stop from the beginning of an exam.

COPING WITH ANXIETY AND STRESS

- Before you go into an exam it is better to avoid discussing anything about it with other candidates. If necessary stay apart on your own.

13

Exam Techniques

First things first

If you are taking examinations through your school or college some of these things will have been organized for you and you will just be told when to turn up. People organizing their own exams should check through *all* the following points.

1. Have you entered for the exam?
2. Do you know where it is taking place?
3. Do you know what time it starts?
4. Do you know how to get there? Do a practice run if necessary so that you can time the journey accurately and know where you have to go.
5. Do you know the format of the paper and how long you should allocate to each question?
6. Do you have everything you need?

- It is a good idea to have two of everything.
- Have everything packed and ready for use in an 'exam bag' which you keep ready just to pick up and go.
- Checklist:

  Information card with your candidate number, exam centre number and telephone number (in case of emergencies)
  Exam timetable
  Pens
  Ink/cartridges
  Sharpened pencils
  Sharpened crayons
  Ruler
  Calculator
  Spare batteries for calculator
  Pencil sharpener

Set square
Protractor
Compasses
Mascot

Taking the paper

The following points cover the basic approach to taking an exam. Practise them in the run-up to the real thing so that they are second nature when you come to take the exam itself.

1. Turn the paper face up, take a deep breath and calm down before you start.
2. Follow instructions accurately.
3. Take time to read carefully through the paper.
4. Give adequate time to choosing which questions you will answer.

- Reading and choosing questions can take up to 10 minutes.
- Underline the questions you want to answer.
- If there is nothing on the paper you like go about it the other way. Cross off the ones you *definitely* cannot do.
- Look at the rest and cross off the ones you would *rather* not do.
- Make your choice from what is left.

5. Make certain you really understood the questions.

- Not answering the actual question set is a major cause of irritation to examiners and of poor marks for candidates.
- Do not rush and make careless mistakes by misunderstanding the question or assuming you know what the examiner is asking.

6. Allocate the correct amount of time to each question or group of questions.

- Some examination papers show time/marks allocated to the different questions or sections. Stick to these guidelines.
- Where no guidelines are given make your own. Add together (a) the time taken to read through the paper and choose the questions, and (b) the time you will need at the end of the examination to check through what you have done (probably about five minutes). Subtract this total from the overall time of the exam, for example, 180 minutes overall exam time minus 15–16 minutes for reading and checking = 164 minutes. Divide the remaining time between the number of questions to be done, for example, 164 minutes divided by four questions is 41 minutes per question.
- Work on practice papers will make you familiar with the examination format so that by the time you get into the examination itself you should know already exactly how long to allocate to each question/section.

7. Decide the order in which you do the questions.

- In maths papers it is usually best to work through in the order on the paper.
- In most other subjects the best rule is:
  > Do your second-best question first to ease yourself in.
  > Do your best question second while you are still fresh and you have got into the swing of things.
  > Do remaining questions in order of preference, finishing on your least favourite question.

8. Note the start and finish times for each question, or group of questions.

- Mark the start and finish times on your exam paper.
- Keep to this timetable to within 1–2 minutes.
- Take off your watch and put it in your direct eyeline so that you can monitor the time easily.

9. Do not start to write until you are sure you have:

- understood the instructions;
- chosen the questions;
- decided the order of the questions;
- marked the times to begin and end questions.

10. Good presentation earns marks.

- Correct spelling, neat handwriting, careful punctuation, accurate working of mathematics, clear diagrams – all these will earn marks. Marks will be lost unnecessarily for sloppy work.
- Imagine you are an examiner checking dozens of papers. Would you have the patience to cope with indecipherable handwriting and careless mistakes?

11. Write the number of the question *not* the full title. Writing the title of the question out in full is time-consuming and unnecessary.
12. Answer the full number of questions required.

- Each question has an allocation of marks. You will usually have been told in class how the questions are weighted (or the number of marks may be stated on the exam paper itself).
- Do not forget what you learned in practice – leave enough time to answer all the questions. Each question not attempted is a definite number of marks lost.

13. Take the full time for each question. Do not be tempted to run over on your 'favourite' question or you may not finish the paper.
14. Use summaries in emergencies.

- If there is not enough time to finish an essay question summarize the remainder in note form to get in as many points as possible.
- This is a last resort, and you should not make a habit of it. However, it is better than leaving points out altogether through lack of time.

15. Do not finish too early.

- Correct planning of the paper and the answers should mean that you use up the entire examination period constructively. There is nothing clever about finishing ahead of time. If you finish very early look at your answer critically. Is there enough detail? Are there enough examples? Have you missed out major points? Have you answered all of the question?
- Spare time should be used for checking spelling, punctuation, facts, working in maths questions, etc.

16. Read through at the end and check for errors.

- You should have left enough time to do this when allocating time to each of the questions.
- Make alterations and additions as neatly as possible.

Multiple choice/multiple response questions

1. There is no need to read the paper through before you start *but* do make sure you have read and understood the instructions.
2. Do not spend a long time on one particular question. The more you get through the better.
3. Go through the paper once doing all the questions you can answer without any serious holdups.
4. Read *all* the options before deciding which is correct. There may be several that come close but only one will be absolutely correct.
5. After you have been through the paper once go back to the beginning trying to work out the answers on the questions causing you problems.

   There are usually some obviously wrong alternatives. Discard these and look carefully at what is left. Which alternative comes nearest to the truth?
6. As a last resort go through the paper a final time and make guesses at those questions you cannot work out logically.

EXAM TECHNIQUES

Never leave multiple choice questions unanswered.

Important note   Do not delude yourself that taking stimulants or tranquillizers will help your exam performance. Rely on your own careful preparation and good sense. There are plenty of stories of students thinking they have turned in a brilliant performance who had in fact written reams of rubbish under the influence of unnecessary pills.

14

After the Exams

Positive thinking

1. Be kind to yourself

Give yourself the reward you have been promising yourself through the course. It doesn't have to be something expensive. The best thing is some guilt-free time off to do something which has nothing whatsoever to do with exams or study.

2. Avoid immediate inquests

Do not go over papers and agonize about the correctness of what you did or did not do.

Try not to talk it over with others. You may make yourself worried for no reason and this could affect other exams you are taking.

When all the exams are finished make a point of avoiding lengthy post-mortems. Explain to friends that you would rather forget about it for a while. The only post-mortems you should allow yourself are constructive appraisals of the exam with your teachers to see if you can learn anything from them for another time.

3. Try to forget about results

It may be many weeks before results of public examinations come through. It is best if you can put them out of your mind for a while and relax after all your efforts (though this is easier said than done).

If you are planning a holiday try and make it soon after the exams finish. If a holiday is not possible perhaps you could go and stay with friends. Alternatively, if you are a student you could try and find a temporary job or get involved in some voluntary work which would keep your mind off your worries.

4. If the results are good

With any luck your hard work and good study habits will be rewarded with satisfactory results. Allow yourself to be pleased, relax and celebrate.

Maybe you will feel inspired to study further. Perhaps you will have enjoyed learning enough to want to learn more just for the pleasure of it.

The attitudes you have acquired about getting organized and applying yourself to specific goals will be useful for the rest of your life, even if you decide not to continue studying.

5. If the results are unsatisfactory

- Try not to give in to gloom and doom. Self-pity is totally unproductive.
- Seek advice. Go through the paper carefully, with a sympathetic teacher if possible.
- Pinpoint your mistakes and learn from them.
- Review your working methods honestly, following the advice given in the book. Have you:

(a) defined your goals?
(b) decided on a positive attitude to study?
(c) assessed your strengths and weaknesses?
(d) chosen subjects wisely?
(e) arranged suitable conditions for studying?
(f) organized work and leisure time sensibly?
(g) practised writing skills?
(h) made well-organized notes?
(i) learned to plan essays?
(j) learned as you went along?
(k) not relied only on last-minute revision?
(l) tackled each exam in a methodical way?

Only you will know how far your lack of success is due to laziness or lack of organization. Don't blame the exam or the examiner.

- Decide right now to put past mistakes behind you.

● Adopt a positive approach to the future.

6. Public exams

Obviously lack of success in public exams is harder to cope with because so often other plans depend on what happens.

It is hard to pick yourself up from a major disappointment and come back fighting. However you can be reassured that when a little time has gone by you will be able to put the results into some sort of perspective and recover your equilibrium. You may even find that in some ways you have benefited and learned from the experience.

Remind yourself that you are not the first person to be disappointed in exam results and you certainly will not be the last.

If possible you should plan to retake exams.

● You will feel better immediately you start to do something positive. You will feel that you are back in control of events.
● Contact teachers, the school office and do whatever is required in order to organize taking exams again.
● With advice from teachers or tutors reorganize plans which hinged on exam results. For example, find out what you must do to reapply for colleges/universities.
● If you would rather move on but want to continue with your studies, make enquiries about colleges which will take you with the marks you have achieved.
● If you want to retake exams but feel a new environment would make this easier start finding out about alternative schools/ colleges

NEVER GIVE UP!

15

How Parents Can Help

Most people taking examinations are schoolchildren and young students. However, the advice given here to parents is relevant to *anyone supporting someone* through study and exams.

1. Be supportive

Exams are a stressful time so show patience and understanding.

2. Be reassuring

Encourage the confidence which is so important for studying successfully. Try not to be critical.

3. Arrange somewhere to study

Make sure there is somewhere private and without distractions where work can be done in peace.

4. Offer practical help

It is rarely a good idea for parents without the necessary qualifications to try and teach their children. However, you can help:

- by making sure candidates know what is expected from them, particularly in GCSE work where each exam has many different parts;
- by getting involved in planning study and revision timetables. Make sure that they fit in with family routine and can be achieved;
- by knowing when to keep out of the way. Don't interfere unnecessarily, it will only contribute to tension and add to the pressure.

5. Watch for warning signs

If there are signs of undue stress (sleeplessness, weeping fits) step in in good time and help prevent them getting out of control (see Chapter 12 on preventing anxiety and stress).

6. Make sure things run smoothly

You can take a lot of the strain out of this particular time by making sure that the student has all the necessary 'support services'. This may mean letting him/her get away without helping out around the house as much as you would normally expect. If you can keep things as stress-free as possible you will make a major contribution to success in the exams.

- Keep a relaxed atmosphere but do not underestimate how important the exams are to the student.
- Keep a discreet eye on the amount of work being done. Try and ensure that enough studying is taking place but remember that it is also important to take time off without feeling guilty.
- Make sure there are regular, sensible meals.
- Make sure other family members are considerate about noise, not tempting the exam candidate away from studies, etc.
- Free the student from as many domestic duties as possible in the run-up to the exams.
- Monitor the amount of sleep and try to prevent all-night working sessions.
- Be available to talk to, especially when things do not seem to be going well. Talking things over can take a lot of the stress out of life.
- Check that arrangements for the exams are quite clear. Does the student know when and where she/he is expected and how to get there?

7. Don't nag

8. Support for parents

Exams can be a strain for parents and friends as well as students.

Ask yourself whether you are contributing to your own stress and that of the student by expecting too much or making too much of the exams. Sometimes parents can let their own competitiveness spill over into their children's lives and give them an added burden.

If you have been allowing yourself to get too anxious take time to think things through. Is any of it the end of the world? Can the exams be taken again if necessary? Will the student's life be totally ruined if the exams are not a big success? Does it matter what other people think? If *you* can get things into perspective you will ease things considerably for the person actually taking the exam.

In some schools parents organize groups to discuss what they can do to help at exam time and to get their own anxieties under control. You may shy away from the idea of talking things over with other people but many people find it helpful so do not dismiss it out of hand. If no group exists why not get a few people together and start one?

9. Arrange something to look forward to

Having a treat lined up for the end of the exams helps put them in perspective. Be sure to have the treat whatever the outcome. You can help best by being a staunch supporter *whatever happens in exams* not by withholding treats as retribution for what you consider to be a poor performance.

16

Useful Information

Publications

Study aids

Many useful study aids are published every year. The best advice is to go and spend some time at a good bookshop or library looking through them. You will probably find a concise guide to exactly the book, topic or project which you need to study.

Some of the new study guides include cassettes as well as books. There are also handy packs of revision cards for topics such as French verbs or basic mathematics.

Although these publications are wonderful back-up material they are no substitute for the confidence that comes from having learned and thoroughly understood a subject yourself.

Among the long-running and well-proven ranges are:

BBC Help Yourself Interactive Packs (GCSE, book and cassette)
Brodies Notes on English Literature
Letts 'Made Simple' range of topic guides
Longman's Revision Guides (GCSE)
Longman's Study Guides
Longman's GCSE Pass Packs (60 minute cassette and booklet) Over 20 GCSE topics available
Macmillan Workout series
Penguin Passnotes
Teach Yourself Study Aids (GCSE)

As basic handbooks for checking that your grammar, punctuation and spelling are correct the following are clear and useful:

Correct English by B. A. Phythian (Teach Yourself Books/ Hodder and Stoughton)

English Spelling by Wileman and Wileman (Harrap, Pocket Book)

English Usage, Spelling and Grammar by John O. E. Clark (Harrap, Pocket Book)

How to Succeed in Written Work and Study (A Handbook for Students in All Subjects in Universities and Colleges) by Richard Ellis and Konrad Hopkins (Collins)

The Pan Dictionary of English Spelling by Martin H. Manser (Pan)

Word Perfect – A Dictionary of Current English Usage by John O. E. Clark (Harrap, Reference)

Computers

If you have access to a computer/word-processor you might like to use Spell Check and Thesaurus software.

Also available, and becoming cheaper all the time, are handheld computers dedicated solely to Spell Checking and Thesaurus. These are small enough to be carried with you.

Diaries

Collins Academic Year Diary

Dictionaries of quotations

The Dictionary of Biographical Quotation by J. Wintle and R. Kenin (Penguin)

Contradictory Quotations (Longman Pocket Companion Series)

Quotations in History by A. and V. Palmer (Harvester Press)

The Dictionary of Modern Quotations by J. M. and M. J. Cohen (Penguin)

The Concise Oxford Dictionary of Quotations (Oxford University Press)

There are many similar books, some with particular themes which might fit in with your own subjects. A visit to the reference library would be well rewarded.

General reference books

Chambers Biographical Dictionary
(short biographies of famous people, living and dead, from throughout the world)

Dictionaries of (among others): Art and Artists, Geography, History, Literary Biography, Saints

The Encyclopaedia Britannica
(a comprehensive general reference work in 30 volumes)
Historic Houses, Castles and Gardens Open to the Public
(British Leisure Publications)
(details of over 1300 houses, castles and gardens)
Museums and Galleries in Great Britain and Ireland
(British Leisure Publications)
(details of over 12 000 museums)

Research by Ann Hoffmann (Adam and Charles Black, 1979)
(intended for writers but a useful guide to sources for university students)

The Times Index
(an index to items published in the *Times*, going back to 1906)
also
Palmer's Index to The Times (1791–1941)

Whitaker's Almanack
('an unparalleled wealth of information about public affairs, government, industry, finance, commerce, social usage and the arts')

Who's Who
(short biographies of famous and influential living people)
also
Out-of-date copies for information on those now dead
also
A whole range of books now available on specific categories, for example, *Who's Who in the Theatre*.

Copies of the syllabus

For copies of the syllabus and specimen exam papers write, detailing what you require, to the appropriate board or professional body. Where possible telephone first to find out current prices.

GCSE and A level boards

London and East Anglian Group

Publications Department,
East Anglian Examination Board,
The Lindens,
139 Lexden Road,
Colchester,
Essex CO3 3RL

Tel: 0206 549595

Midland Examining Association

Publications Department,
University of Cambridge Local Examinations Syndicate,
Syndicate Buildings,
1 Hills Road,
Cambridge
CB1 2EV

Tel: 0223 61111

Northern Examining Association

Write to your local board

Associated Lancashire Schools Examining Board,
12 Harter Street,
Manchester M1 6HL

Tel: 061 228 0084

North Regional Examinations Board,
Wheatfield Road,
Westerhope,
Newcastle upon Tyne NE5 5JZ

Tel: 091 286 2711

North West Regional Examinations Board,
Orbit House,
Albert Street,
Eccles,
Manchester M30 0WL

Tel: 061 788 9521

Yorkshire and Humberside Regional Examinations Board,
Harrogate Office,
31–33 Springfield Avenue,
Harrogate HG1 2HW

Tel: 042 356 6991

Joint Matriculation Board,
Manchester M15 6EU

Tel: 061 273 2565

Northern Ireland Schools Examinations Council

Publications Department,
Beechill House,
42 Beechill Road,
Belfast BT8 4RS

Tel: 0232 704666

Southern Examining Group

**Publications Department,
Stag Hill House,
Guildford GU2 5XJ**

Tel: 0483 503123

Welsh Joint Education Committee

**Publications Department,
245 Western Avenue,
Cardiff CF5 2YX**

Tel: 0222 561 231